MONTANA HISTORIC PLACES

ON THE NATIONAL REGISTER

From Banks and Barns to Bridges and Battlefields

MICHAEL OBER

Montana Historic Places

ON THE NATIONAL REGISTER

From Banks and Barns to Bridges and Battlefields

MICHAEL OBER

2022
Mountain Press Publishing Company
Missoula, Montana

First Printing, February 2022

Cover photo: Granite Park Chalet in Glacier National Park. —Photo by Steve Woodruff

Maps constructed by Chelsea M. Feeney (cmcfeeney.com)

Library of Congress Cataloging-in-Publication

Data\ Names: Ober, Michael, 1948- author.
Title: Montana historic places on the National Register : from banks and barns to bridges and battlefields / Michael J. Ober.
Description: Missoula : Mountain Press Publishing Company, 2022. | Includes bibliographical references and index. | Summary: "More than one thousand locations in Montana are listed on the National Register of Historic Places, from venerable mansions and hotels to less traditional sites of battlefields and buffalo jumps. This sampler of fifty carefully selected sites highlights the broad geographic and topical range of Montana's historic places, from iconic to unconventional. Beautiful color photographs of each historic place in its modern setting accompany the site narrative. Residents and tourists alike will learn about Montana's colorful history as they tour the backroads to many little-known but historically significant sites"—Provided by publisher.
Identifiers: LCCN 2021049841 | ISBN 9780878427062 (paperback)
Subjects: LCSH: Historic sites—Montana. | Historic buildings—Montana. | National Register of Historic Places.
Classification: LCC F732 .O24 2022 | DDC 978.6–dc23/eng/20211018
LC record available at https://lccn.loc.gov/2021049841

PRINTED IN THE UNITED STATES

MP Mountain Press
PUBLISHING COMPANY
P.O. Box 2399 • Missoula, MT 59806 • 406-728-1900
800-234-5308 • info@mtnpress.com
www.mountain-press.com

PREFACE AND ACKNOWLEDGMENTS

The preparation of a book draws upon many different resources and individuals. In the building process, people assemble themselves for a common goal, marshal their talents, and produce an item for public consumption and a celebratory moment.

To the following partners I owe my earnest thanks. John Boughton of the Montana State Historic Preservation Office, for his responses to my queries and keen knowledge of Montana's expansive range of historic places. Numerous history-minded individuals, government agencies, organizations, and institutions stepped in to provide images of sites in their towns and countrysides. Steve Woodruff, no stranger to writing and photography and whose many vivid photographs are found on these pages, started this whole adventure over a casual dinner in Missoula, when he broached the subject of writing a book about interesting places in Montana listed on the National Register of Historic Places (NRHP). I gathered much of the detailed information in this book from the NRHP documentation. Finally, and most importantly, my wife, Alanna, who comforted me when I was discouraged and dedicated endless moments of editing and proofreading along the way. Thank you all.

During my many years teaching Montana history to college sophomores, I conducted an overnight field trip to Fort Benton, Montana's storied birthplace, with its numerous historic signs, fine interpretive center, and museums. There, amid all its richness, we gathered for a customary group photo of everyone placing their hands on the stucco cladding of the original fort's guardhouse—Montana's oldest building. We stayed at the oldest operating hotel in the state, the Grand Union, listed on the NRHP and whose phone number ends with 1882, a nod to its birth year. The aim, of course, was to connect the students to some physical evidence of our shared past. Similarly, on the bluffs overlooking the town and fabled Missouri River, I had them pick up a handful of dirt and reminded them that they held a piece of the Louisiana Purchase—thank you, Thomas Jefferson. A teaching moment. I have no idea what impact those gestures had on their young lives. Maybe in their later years, memories will emerge and they will reflect on those events. But I will always believe this: places matter.

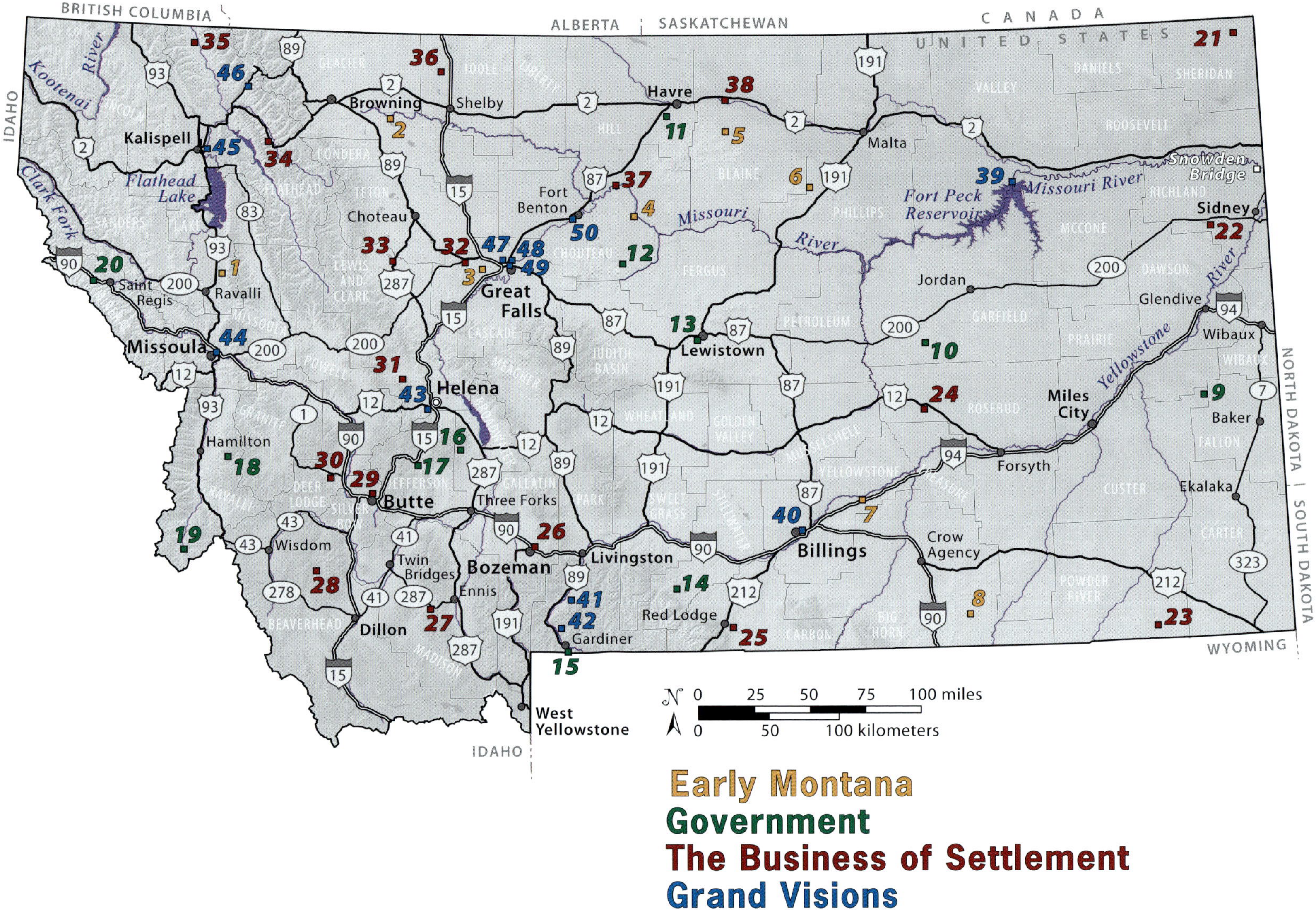

BRITISH COLUMBIA
ALBERTA
SASKATCHEWAN
CANADA
UNITED STATES
IDAHO
NORTH DAKOTA
SOUTH DAKOTA
WYOMING
Kalispell
Browning
Shelby
Havre
Malta
Choteau
Fort Benton
Great Falls
Helena
Missoula
Saint Regis
Ravalli
Hamilton
Butte
Three Forks
Wisdom
Twin Bridges
Bozeman
Ennis
Dillon
Livingston
Gardiner
West Yellowstone
Red Lodge
Billings
Crow Agency
Lewistown
Jordan
Glendive
Wibaux
Sidney
Miles City
Forsyth
Baker
Ekalaka
Flathead Lake
Kootenai River
Clark Fork
Missouri River
Fort Peck Reservoir
Yellowstone River
Snowden Bridge
0 25 50 75 100 miles
0 50 100 kilometers
Early Montana
Government
The Business of Settlement
Grand Visions

CONTENTS

Preface and Acknowledgments v
Introduction 1

EARLY MONTANA 5
1. Fort Connah Site 6
2. Two Medicine Fight Site 8
3. First Peoples Buffalo Jump 10
4. Citadel Rock 12
5. Chief Joseph Battleground of the Bear's Paw 14
6. Lookout Cave 16
7. Pompeys Pillar 18
8. Rosebud Battlefield 20

GOVERNMENT 23
9. Cottonwood Creek Bridge 24
10. Hornaday Camp 26
11. Fort Assiniboine 28
12. Square Butte Jail 30
13. Lewistown Satellite Airfield 32
14. Dean School 34
15. Roosevelt Arch 36
16. Eagle Guard Station 38
17. Montana State Training School 40
18. Gird Point Lookout 42
19. Alta Ranger Station 44
20. Savenac Nursery 46

THE BUSINESS OF SETTLEMENT 49
21. Comertown 50
22. Burgess Garage 52
23. Cross Ranch Headquarters 54
24. Jersey Lilly Saloon 56
25. Smith Mine District 58
26. Northern Pacific–Story Mill Historic District 59
27. Virginia City 62
28. Elkhorn-Coolidge Ghost Town 64
29. Butte-Anaconda Historic District 66
30. Anaconda Smokestack 68
31. Methodist-Episcopal Church of Marysville 70
32. J. C. Adams Stone Barn 72
33. Gilman State Bank 74
34. Izaak Walton Inn 76
35. Wurtz Homestead 78
36. Kevin Depot 80
37. Virgelle Mercantile and Bank 82
38. Dave's Texaco 84

GRAND VISIONS 87
39. Fort Peck Theatre 88
40. Moss Mansion 90
41. Chico Hot Springs 92
42. OTO Homestead and Dude Ranch 94
43. Cathedral of Saint Helena 96
44. University Apartments 98
45. Conrad Mansion 100
46. *DeSmet* Tour Boat 102
47. Chicago, Milwaukee, and St. Paul Passenger Depot 104
48. Charles M. Russell House and Studio 106
49. Tenth Street Bridge 108
50. Grand Union Hotel 109

Epilogue: Snowden Bridge 112
Bibliography 114
Index 116

Garnet, a ghost town from the gold mining days. —PHOTO BY STEVE WOODRUFF

INTRODUCTION

In Missoula's iconic Rockin Rudy's store is a T-shirt with a colorful design and this legend: "Missoula Montana. A place. Sort of." In its own abstract way, the legend defines what the town is. Or isn't. A few blocks away there is a small aluminum sign declaring the vintage University Apartments as being officially enshrined on the National Register of Historic Places (NRHP). In a more defining way, this designation celebrates a location that has clarity and meaning. The significance of the apartment complex's architecture, and the role it played in the growth of the Missoula city core, landed it, with more than one million other places across the nation, on the NRHP.

Chances are, there is a similar place of national historic importance in your town, your neighborhood, your countryside. They are out there. Everywhere. In Vermont it may be an historic covered bridge. In Pennsylvania it may be a textile mill converted to townhomes. In Montana it's likely to be an abandoned silver mine moldering against the mountain slope from which it once drew its wealth.

Approximately eighty thousand NRHP sites across the nation are individual properties, whereas others are categorized as "historic districts" or "contributing" places. Many are vacant buildings, many are occupied by owners and residents, and many are awaiting new occupants, such as commercial buildings that can be used as retail sites. A great many, though, are merely places on a map where a noteworthy event occurred.

Montana has more than 1,100 locations listed on the NRHP, with the number growing each year. That's enough to have one or more in just about every community in the state, with plenty left over to spill out into Montana's sprawling 93 million acres. Flathead County leads the list with 147 sites; Teton County has only 1, its county courthouse, built in 1906. From durable brick-and-stone courthouses and banks to crumbling

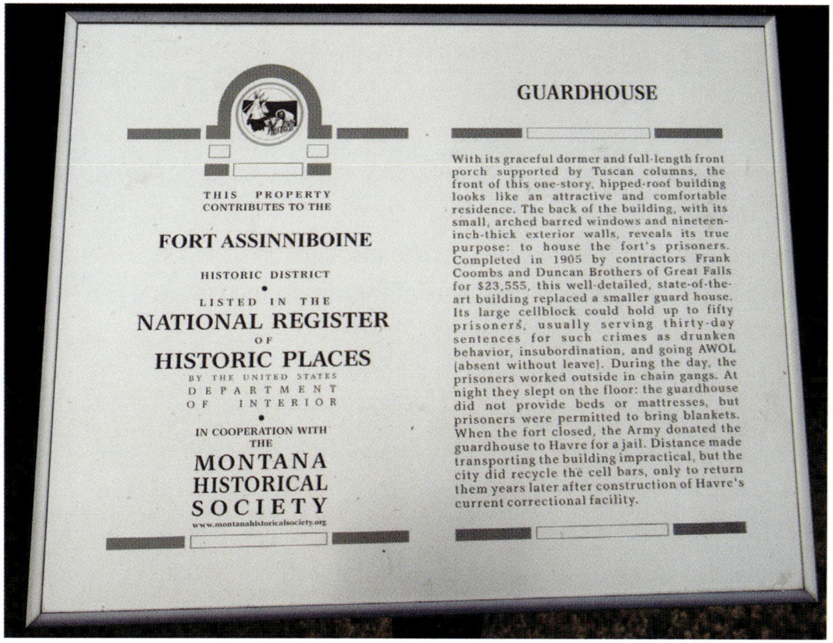

A place on the NRHP has a small plaque announcing its importance.
—PHOTO BY STEVE WOODRUFF

log homesteads, there's plenty to explore. Some are obvious and in heavily populated areas; some require windshield time on tough rural roads and a certain perseverance. Finding these sites is sort of like a find-me-if-you-can geocaching for history buffs. And each has its own unique tale to tell.

Not all sites are immortal or for all time. The list is a fluid one. Some are destined to crumble as age and neglect dictate their destiny. Montana's sites range from eye candy to lowbrow. There are "trophy" sites like the Big Hole Battlefield National Monument, and there are older, sometimes unassuming residential properties down the street in just about every town that were built by famous architects or were occupied by notable townspeople. In between there's a collection of rusty bridges, charming churches, elegant courthouses, rustic ranger stations, brick banks, magnificent mansions, and a modest sampling of homesteads and barns. There's even a dude ranch, gas stations, and a few bars.

Montana has its share of oddities on the list, of course. In what's left of the homestead town of Lambert there's a garage that doubled as a medical office. It, like most of the list's remote places, might draw only a handful of the curious each year—some on purpose, but most by serendipity or accident. And then there are the vintage wooden tour boats in Glacier National Park, floating "places" familiar to thousands of park visitors.

A few places provoke some head-scratching. There's a creamery, water pumping stations, abandoned airway beacons, a street underpass, an oil field sign, a radio station, a phone line, and my favorite, "Froggie's Stopping Place on the Whoop-Up Trail." Observers may well ponder the reasoning behind nominating places that seem to have no particular historic connections. "How did this place make the list?" one might ask. If you dig deeper, read the inscription on the plaque, and open an imaginative mind, the real rationale always emerges, no matter how mundane the site may seem at first glance. There's always a story. Considered from any angle, these sites have a way of getting our history right.

The nominating and awarding process is pretty simple. To begin, a nominating person or agency must prepare a standardized form and submit it to the central offices of the National Register of Historic Places in Washington, DC. The agency is part of the National Park Service. Most nomination forms are ushered through their respective state's historic preservation office first, where they are scrutinized for accuracy and importance. In the words of the National Park Service:

> To be considered eligible, a property must meet the National Register Criteria for Evaluation. This involves examining the property's age, integrity, and significance.
>
> • Age and Integrity: Is the property old enough to be considered historic (generally at least 50 years old) and does it still look much the way it did in the past?
>
> • Significance: Is the property associated with events, activities, or developments that were important in the past? With the lives of people who were important in the past? With significant architectural history, landscape history, or engineering achievements? Does it have the potential to yield information through archeological investigation about our past?

That's it. Once on the list, owners may order a metal plaque to affix to the structure or site. Benefits also accrue to the owners in the form of:

- Federal preservation grants for planning and rehabilitation
- Federal investment tax credits
- Preservation easements to nonprofit organizations
- International building code fire and life safety code alternatives

The documentation varies widely. In the case of the remote Cottonwood Creek Bridge in Fallon County, the nomination documents number twenty-three pages, including bibliographies, detailed narratives, diagrams, charts, a glossary, and an exhaustive history of timber auto bridges. John Axline, of the Montana Department of Transportation and the avowed guru of all things involving transportation history of the state, prepared the documents in 2014 to celebrate what might seem to some as just an ordinary bridge on a rural gravel road. For the most part, Montana's sites are dominated by these built landscapes, shaped by human hands. Others, in smaller numbers, evoke natural terrain features. Still others, mostly private residences, contain more brief narrative support.

This book offers a sampling of the many official NRHP sites in Montana. They are grouped in four broad topical categories: early Montana, government, the business of settlement, and grand visions. Out of respect for privacy, I didn't include many of the private residences, occupied or vacant, that make up a great number of the state's sites. Since Montana is such a large state, geography played a role in the selection process. I wanted to make sure that the sites represented as much of the state as possible. I hope you enjoy some of these deeper stories of our state, place by place, event by event, encapsulated by these landmarks.

The Swiftcurrent fire lookout in Glacier National Park was built in 1936. —PHOTO BY STEVE WOODRUFF

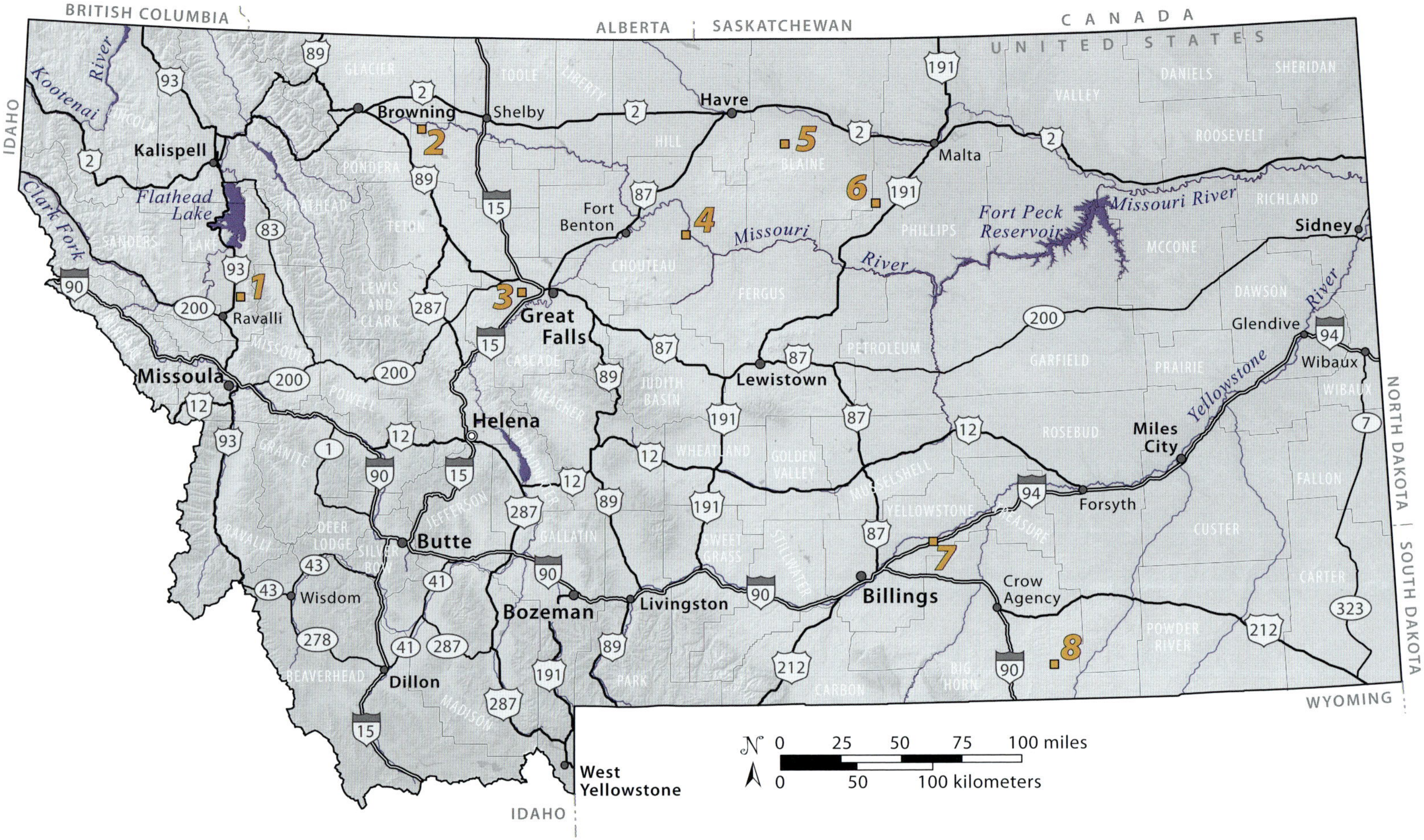

1 Fort Connah
2 Two Medicine Fight Site
3 First People's Buffalo Jump
4 Citadel Rock
5 Chief Joseph Battleground of the Bear's Paw
6 Lookout Cave
7 Pompeys Pillar
8 Rosebud Battlefield

EARLY MONTANA

"Montana is Indian country," Carl Davis proclaims in his landmark book, *Six Hundred Generations*. "It has been so since the arrival of the first hunter-gatherers from northeast Asia near the end of the last great Ice Age, some 15,000 years ago." We tend to think of "history," as it relates to Indian societies, as revolving around conflicts with white European expansionists during the territorial period. As Davis makes clear, the history of these cultures is much deeper, spanning thousands of years before written history and that first contact with Europeans. This chapter acquaints readers with identifiable sites in Montana associated with the state's first inhabitants and its early Euro-American explorers, trappers, and soldiers, both before first contact between the groups and through the middle nineteenth-century clash of cultures.

Judith Landing Historic District on the Missouri River encompasses a variety of places from early Montana, including Native American sites, a Lewis and Clark campsite from 1805, a fur-trading fort from 1844, and the outcrop where Ferdinand Hayden in 1855 collected the first identified dinosaur fossils in the Western Hemisphere. —PHOTO BY STEVE WOODRUFF

1

FORT CONNAH SITE

47°24′20″N 114°05′14″W

Along US 93 north of St. Ignatius in Lake County

Being the first of something figures largely in a site's placement on the NRHP. Accordingly, putting Fort Connah on the register made simple sense in 1968 when it was nominated. Constructed in 1846, it is the oldest structure west of the Continental Divide in Montana. That said, there is lively debate about what is Montana's oldest structure, because Fort Benton, east of the divide, is said to have been built in the same year.

Both forts trace their beginnings to the fur trade era. As the frontier equivalents of convenience stores, they were designed to be commercial trading posts, not military facilities. At a time when Britain and the United States were competing for market share, the battle for fur supremacy was on. All lands west of the divide in today's Montana were claimed by the British Crown, who chartered the venerable Hudson's Bay Company to exploit the riches found there. The company built Fort Connah in today's Mission Valley to solidify their claim. Conversely, the rival American Fur Company established Fort Benton as their own "fist in the wilderness" as a competing trade outlet. Fort Connah was the Hudson's Bay Company's last effort to thwart the aggressive American traders who were looking to establish themselves west of the divide.

The remaining building at Fort Connah, representing the final physical presence of British interests in Montana, is a good example of the channeled log construction used widely by the British at their trading outposts. Since there have been no formal archaeological excavations at the site, it is not clear where or how many other buildings were part of the original trading post, but historians believe there were no more than four. The foundations of any adjacent structures are likely buried nearby. The two-story, one-room log building has undergone numerous renovations in the past 175 years, both during occupancy and post-occupancy periods. The Fort Connah Restoration Society has been responsible for the recent work.

A noncontiguous parcel of land located less than half a mile east of the log building is also part the historical site. It contains the graves of Angus MacDonald, the original Hudson's Bay factor, his Native American wife, and more than twenty-one other people associated with the earliest days at the post.

—PHOTO BY STEVE WOODRUFF

Angus MacDonald headstone. —PHOTO BY STEVE WOODRUFF

Fireplace in cabin. —PHOTO BY STEVE WOODRUFF

2

TWO MEDICINE FIGHT SITE

48°28′8N 112°28′W

Along the Two Medicine River southeast of Browning in Pondera County

The Two Medicine Fight Site is not an easy place to get to, but that's what makes it a rewarding find. Southeast of Browning by 24 miles of gravel road, this remote spot beneath the wrinkled and weathered branches of a cottonwood cluster marks a moment of history of no small consequence that occurred more than two hundred years ago. Here, adjacent to the Two Medicine River, Meriwether Lewis, brothers Reuben and Joseph Fields, and George Droulliard clashed with a band of eight Blackfeet Indians on July 26, 1806.

The small party of American explorers, traveling separately from the main Corps of Discovery, had been on a lengthy reconnaissance north of the Missouri River, exploring the furthest northern reaches of the Louisiana Purchase. This venture was critical to their mission because the explorers sought to claim as much land as they could for President Thomas Jefferson's vision to expand the nation's boundaries. Up to this point the expedition, now returning home after having crossed the continent once, had a flawless record of harmonious relationships with the countless Native Americans they had met along the way.

Upon becoming aware of each other late in the day on the 25th, the Americans and Blackfeet apprehensively approached each other on the open plains, and using Droulliard as the interpreter, the two parties agreed to encamp together under the trees alongside the river. After an evening of interpreted dialogue, Lewis and his men awoke at daybreak to discover that the Indians, likely young teenaged boys, were stealing their horses and guns. During the brief ensuing fight Lewis shot and killed one of the Indians, and Reuben Fields stabbed and killed another. With their horses recovered, and fearing there were other Blackfeet nearby, they mounted a furious ride back to the Missouri River, pushing their horses "as hard as they would bear." Riding through the night with only brief rest stops, they covered nearly 110 miles in under 14 hours in what would become Montana's first endurance ride. At the Missouri, they reunited with the rest of the expedition members and continued their journey downriver. Although they recovered their horses and guns, they left behind festering disharmony and suspicions. To the white explorers and settlers who followed on the heels of the Corps over the next one hundred years, the Blackfeet Nation became the feared raiders of Montana's northern plains. And to the Indians, the white people were unwelcome intruders.

Lewis may have had something to do with this strained relationship. He was a brilliant yet troubled soul prone to fits of impulsiveness. During their hasty departure from the fight

—PHOTO BY KENT SCHLAWIN

site, Lewis hung a peace medallion around the neck of the Indian boy he had just killed so that others might be "informed [of] who we were." The medallion bore the image of Thomas Jefferson on one side and two hands clasped in a handshake on the other. an ominous calling card, possibly laced with a defiant "new sheriff in town" message.

Today, the same unassuming clump of cottonwood trees marks the exact spot where the parties camped. It is now encircled with a wooden fence and commemorated with an interpretive sign. The site joined the NRHP in 1970. Access is through Blackfeet Trust lands and is challenging terrain. A Blackfeet Tribal Recreation Permit and guide are required.

3

FIRST PEOPLES BUFFALO JUMP

47°28′46″N 111°31′27″W

Near Ulm in Cascade County

The first residents of what would become Montana migrated to the region about fifteen thousand years ago. These travelers from Eurasia are rightfully considered the state's original citizens. They were foot nomads for thousands of years before their ancestors acquired horses just three hundred years ago.

These early peoples were wanderers of the Front Range of the Rockies. Long before bows and arrows and firearms, with crude hunting implements they preyed on just about anything they could bring down for food, clothing, and tools. While ambush and slow pursuit were their preferred methodology for killing large animals, such as woolly mammoths, their descendants developed the unique and convenient tactic of driving bison herds over a cliff edge to procure food.

The First Peoples Buffalo Jump was used extensively for this purpose beginning around nine hundred years ago. Evidence of this is expressed in the bone bed at the foot of the mile-long cliff. More than 13 feet deep, the bed contains the remains of thousands of buffalo. This site was one of Montana's first butcher shops.

More recently, these compacted bone beds were quarried for sandstone and mined for phosphorous used for fertilizer and explosive manufacturing. The state of Montana acquired the site after World War II and began a lengthy series of land swaps, donations, and transfers that led to the creation of the first preserved buffalo jump in the state. Amateur archaeologists began interpreting the site in the 1950s and uncovered the evidence about the importance of the site. Montana designated the area a state monument to prevent desecration and scavenging.

In February 2000, the site was changed from a state monument to a state park and named Ulm Pishkun Buffalo Jump State Park. Interpretive trails and signs describe a place used as a supply depot by humans for thousands of years, and the handsome 2.2-million-dollar visitor center was the first *pishkun* ("deep blood kettle" in the Blackfeet language) visitor center in both the state of Montana and the nation.

There are only two other preserved buffalo jump sites in Montana. First Peoples is considered one of the largest buffalo jumps in North America. For Montanans, it commemorates the long and enduring story of the lives and culture of the state's first residents.

—PHOTO BY STEVE WOODRUFF

4

CITADEL ROCK

47°49′52″N 110°04′28″W

On the Missouri River east of Fort Benton in Chouteau County

Citadel Rock is an unchanged, towering stone landmark that's well documented in Missouri River lore. While toiling upriver in dugout canoes and pirogues, the Lewis and Clark Expedition first encountered it in 1805. Captain William Clark noted it as "a high steep black rock riseing [*sic*] from the waters edge." Three decades later, the prominent spire became a waypoint for fur trappers navigating the river. In 1833, during the great fur trade era, German explorer Prince Maximilian of Wied-Neuwied, on his epic voyage to Fort McKenzie, noted it on August 6. It was on that day that the talented artist Karl Bodmer, who was accompanying him, sketched the rock, forever making it a famous Missouri River natural feature. And even later, Citadel Rock became a landmark to steamboat travelers and was noted on most river maps of that era. Diaries of riverboat passengers bound for Fort Benton often made note of the rock, and captains were known to reduce speed and even "lay by" near it so that its majestic height could be admired.

Citadel Rock is anchored along the river due to its resistance to erosion; it is a former magma core from an ancient volcano. The dark igneous rock stands apart from the surrounding white sandstones that line the river channel. At a narrow point in the river's flow, it rises sharply more than 100 feet above the water's surface.

Declared a state monument in 1967, it has been an NRHP landmark since 1974. Just as in days gone by, this inspiring landform of this Wild and Scenic River corridor is accessible only by watercraft.

—PHOTO BY CHUCK HANEY, ©chuckhaney.com

5

CHIEF JOSEPH BATTLEGROUND OF THE BEAR'S PAW

48°22'39"N 109°12'26"W

15 miles south of Chinook in Blaine County

Forty-Five miles south of the Canadian line, in Blaine County, Snake Creek barely makes a flow. It meanders, twists, and curves in a brush-filled coulee on the bare plains, marking the slow passage of time. It is an unlikely place for a military defensive position, and yet more than seven hundred Nez Perce Indians put up a valiant fight here for six cold autumn days and nights. In this place, now enshrined as an NRHP site and managed by the National Park Service as a historic battlefield, the remarkable retreat of the nontreaty Nez Perce ended in 1877. Pursued by the unrelenting US military, they fell just short of the security of the Canadian "Medicine Line."

Whether they thought they had reached the safety of Canada, where Sitting Bull's band of Sioux had fled the year before after Little Big Horn, or they were too exhausted to continue their 1,700-mile, three-month retreat across Idaho and Montana, they halted to rest. They made camp, failing to see their peril until it was too late. Then the soldiers arrived. Then it began to snow.

In filthy rags and tattered blankets, the Nez Perce fought hard against poor odds. After an initial attack on the encampment, Captain Nelson Miles and his troops encircled the Indians and began a desultory siege that spanned from September 30 to October 5. Somehow, 98 warriors and 200 women and children made it through the perimeter and escaped into Canada. The 87 men, 184 women, and 147 children that remained under the leadership of Chief Joseph, however, surrendered, too hungry, cold, and weary to endure any more suffering.

Today the battlefield, part of Nez Perce National Historical Park south of Chinook, is almost as lonely and isolated as it was in 1877. It includes a parking lot, picnic tables, interpretive signs, and a mile-long trail that overlooks the Indian encampment. Along the route are signs marking Indian lodge sites, rifle pits, and bullet-scarred rocks. Besides these markers of historic human events, the landscape is virtually undisturbed . . . and hauntingly quiet.

—PHOTOS BY STEVE WOODRUFF

6

LOOKOUT CAVE

Phillips County—Location Restricted

In the faraway reaches of the Little Rocky Mountains is the entrance to a church sanctuary that dates to the archaic period, or meso-Indian period, which spans from 8,000 to 1,000 years BCE. Some of the archaeological evidence in the cave, however, is more recent, dating to as late as 1800. Regardless of the age of the cave's relics, archaeologists have clearly identified Lookout Cave as one of Montana's first places of worship. While European colonists clinging to the East Coast were struggling to assert their own brand of religious freedom, church was already in session in Montana.

The kinds of artifacts found, and the lack of hearths, household "litter," and stone manufacturing debris, tell archaeologists that this was an unusual ceremonial cave. It is thought to have been a place for leaving offerings or conducting private ceremonies. Scattered on the floor of the cave's two chambers are thousands of perishable items made of wood, bone, feather, shell, and sinew. Such relics are frequently associated with offerings. Also found are fragmented arrow shafts, bone worked into beads, an incised fossil shell shaped into a necklace pendant, fragments of a pipe, and a wooden flute carved to look like an animal. On the walls there are twenty rock art panels composed of a myriad of finger lines and hand smears. They show human stick figures on vision quests, flying humans, snakes, skeletons, and hand lines connected to ceremonial activities, all locked in time like flies in amber. The wall paintings may have been symbols for rituals or songs, or renderings of visions experienced during a trance or a vision quest. In nominating Lookout Cave to the NRHP, archaeologists explained:

> The lack of warfare and hunting portrayed in the rock art indicates these were not the focus of the rituals conducted in this cave, and the points and arrow shafts in the deposits were likely left as offerings or as parts of shrines for safe passage to or for use in the next world rather than as requests for conquests in war or success in hunting in this world.

Lookout Cave, like other caves in which spiritual activities took place, faces east, offering an unrestricted view of the surrounding countryside (from which the cave derives its name) and the rising sun. "Spiritual" caves such as this are typically found on inaccessible mountain slopes requiring strenuous climbs, and Lookout Cave is no exception. It's located on BLM public land. Out of concern for safety, vandalism, and sensitivity to local native tribes, the cave is closed to the public, but the BLM can arrange for limited access.

Archeologists began exploring Lookout Cave in 1963. Their findings, the artifacts and evidence, tell of the early human need to make offerings and to acknowledge a higher spiritual power—a need that persists for many people in modern times. For thousands of years, then, Lookout Cave was a destination for humans to engage in shamanic activities, vision quests, fertility rituals, hunting magic, and burial ceremonies, but not for human dwelling.

—PHOTO COURTESY BUREAU OF LAND MANAGEMENT

7

POMPEYS PILLAR

45°59′44″N 108°00′17″W

Along the Yellowstone River in Yellowstone County

Montana's earliest recorded evidence of graffiti is etched on a prominent sandstone bluff looking out over the lower Yellowstone River. It was a hot July day in 1806 when William Clark, of the Lewis and Clark Expedition, climbed up on the hulking stone prominence and used his knife to leave the simple inscription:

W Clark July 25, 1806

That evening in camp, Clark made this entry in his ledger:

> At 4 PM arrived at the remarkable rock situated in an extensive bottom on the Stard. Side of the river and 250 paces from it. thick rock I ascended and from it's top had a most extensive view in every direction. This rock which I shall call Pompy's Tower is 200 feet high and 400 paces in secumpherance and only axcessible on one Side which is from the N.E. the other parts of it being a perpendicular clift of lightish coloured gritty rock . . . The natives have ingraved on the face of this rock the figures of animals . . . near which I marked my name and the day of the month & year

It is still believed to be the only physical evidence in existence that the expedition was ever in Montana.

Though not known for frivolous actions, William Clark nevertheless followed a strong impulse to leave some kind of calling card as evidence of his presence, as he and his crew hurried downriver toward home. With him in the return party were Sacajawea and her infant son, Jean Baptiste Charbonneau, whom Clark had nicknamed "Pomp" after he had developed an affection for the youngest member of the expedition.

The sandstone bluff's history runs even deeper than Clark's graffiti. Indians had used the bluff as a signal tower and a message board well before Lewis and Clark passed through what would be Montana. Clark even noted this in his journal, observing that the walls bore Indian petroglyphs. Being the expedition's map maker and surveyor, Clark recorded that the pillar was at the exact intersection of the 46th parallel and the 108th meridian, making it a natural landmark for successive explorers and surveys.

Thus, Clark was not the first nor the last person to leave his mark on this famous bluff. Pompeys Pillar has been a signpost for thousands of years.

—PHOTO COURTESY BUREAU OF LAND MANAGEMENT

8

ROSEBUD BATTLEFIELD

45°13′17″N 106°59′21″W

Along State Highway 314 in Big Horn County

As part of the great Sioux campaign of 1876, General George Crook and his 1,300 mounted infantry and cavalry took to the field on June 17 in southwest Montana to confront the Sioux and Cheyenne, who had refused to confine themselves to reservations that summer. Crook had pushed his soldiers hard the previous night, marching 35 miles before pausing at a broad bowl alongside Rosebud Creek. Then, out of nowhere, Crazy Horse struck.

Crook wrongly thought that the Indians were defending a nearby village, so he dispatched Captain Anson Mills north, both to attack the "village" and to draw the Indians away from his position. Instead of villagers they encountered a full-on offensive force of fighters, each riding a trail horse and leading a war pony. Estimated at 700 to 1,500 strong, and bent on protecting their homeland, these Cheyenne and Sioux were likely the finest and fiercest light cavalry on the northern plains at the time.

Both sides charged, retreated, mounted, dismounted, attacked, and defended numerous strategic positions on the ridges and hills alongside Rosebud Creek during the daylong fight. Both sides laid down relentless and ineffectual fire, more annoying than telling in its accuracy. Archeologists, who have excavated shell casings at the dozens of warrior firing positions, estimate that the Indians used no fewer than thirteen different firearms, most inaccurate and of inferior quality. Only the mule-mounted infantry, armed with Henry repeating .44-caliber rifles, had much success. For all the shots fired, only ten soldiers died, whereas Indian casualties have never been accurately determined.

Though this battle was the largest assemblage, at one place and at one time, of US cavalry and Indian combatants in American history, neither faction gained any tactical advantages that day. The Indians withdrew from the field at about 4 p.m., and Crook and his men turned back south to link up with and resupply from his 106-strong wagon train that was 50 miles behind him and his forward force. Many of the mules were converted to a travois caravan to carry more than 22 wounded soldiers. Days later, Crook limped back to Wyoming Territory. He was done with the Great Sioux War of 1876.

Historians have long speculated on whether Crook's retreat, and, subsequently, his inability to rendezvous with Lt. Col. George A. Custer, made any difference in the more spectacular

PHOTO BY ANDY AUSTIN, MONTANA FISH, WILDLIFE, AND PARKS

Battle of the Little Big Horn eight days later. It is quite certain, however, that the engagement at Rosebud Creek emboldened the Indians and solidified Crazy Horse as an able tactician who was more than a match for the US Calvary.

Rosebud Battlefield, tucked away on a Montana back road and not on the way to anywhere, has changed little over the ensuing years. Given the pristine and nearly undisturbed landscape, West Point cadets use the battlefield to study tactics and deployment strategies associated with mobile forces on challenging terrain. Listed on the NRHP in 1972 and designated a National Historic Landmark in 2008, the battlefield is preserved in a 3,000-acre state park.

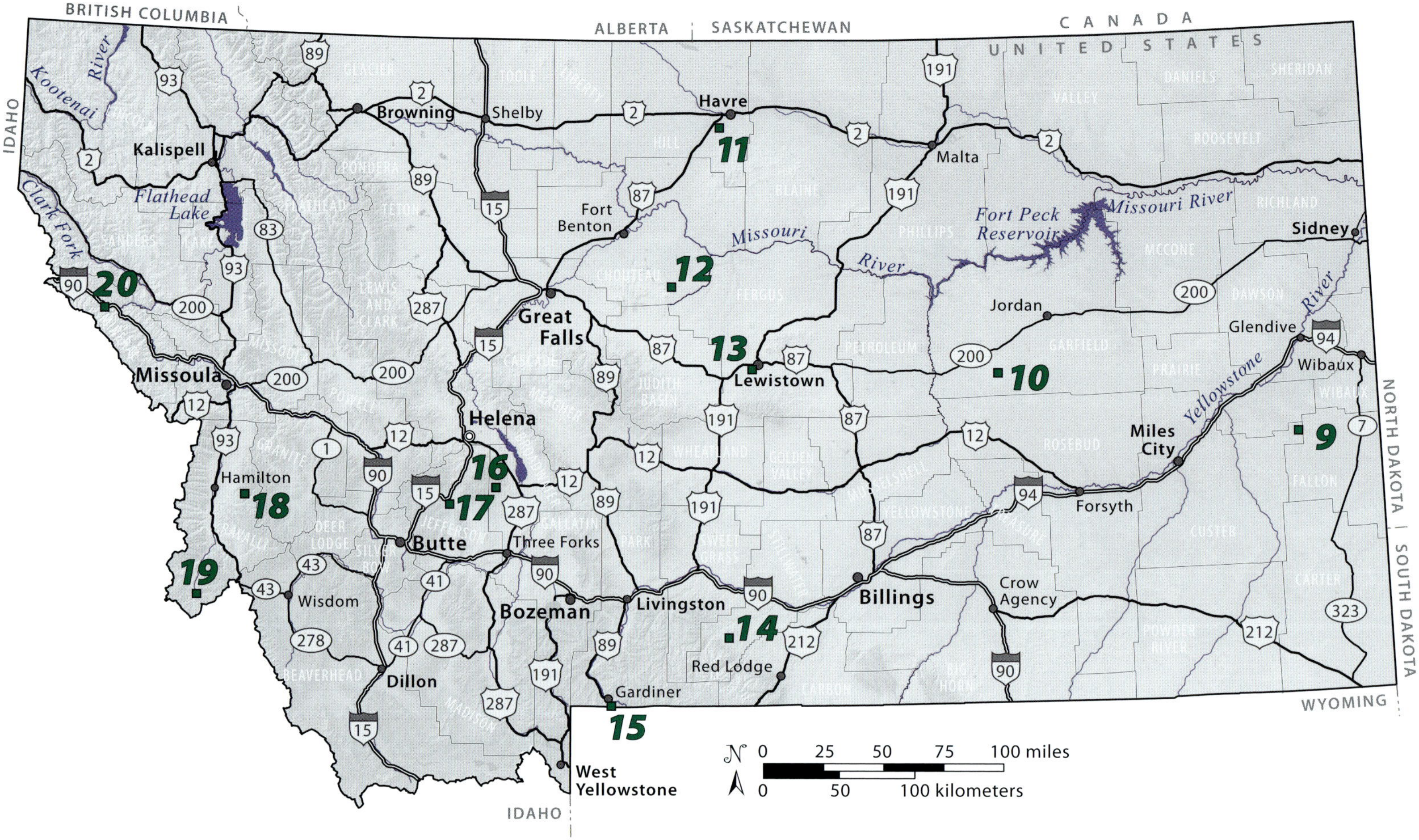

9 Cottonwood Creek Bridge
10 Hornaday Camp
11 Fort Assiniboine
12 Square Butte Jail
13 Lewistown Satellite Airfield
14 Dean School
15 Roosevelt Arch
16 Eagle Guard Station
17 Montana School of Deaf & Dumb
18 Gird Point Lookout
19 Alta Ranger Station
20 Savenac Nursery

Government

With more than 33 million acres of public land in Montana, local, county, state, and federal governments loom large in the lives of the state's citizens. When it comes to identifying and enshrining historic sites influenced by governmental agencies, there are plenty to choose from. Forts, courthouses, jails, schools, airports, bridges, fire lookouts, and libraries are sprinkled all over the NRHP map of Montana. Next to private homes, governmental historic sites dominate the list.

The distinct themes with governmental historic sites are utility and need. Bridges and post offices are not typically associated with architectural splendor in the way that posh—and often garish—private mansions are. The charm of a vintage public school in Montana comes from the needs it served rather than its beauty. In this chapter, we'll explore places that emerged from Montanans' need for safety, stability, and permanence.

The Deer Lodge County Courthouse in Anaconda was built in 1898. —PHOTO BY STEVE WOODRUFF

9

COTTONWOOD CREEK BRIDGE

46°27′24″N 104°47′19″W

On Ismay Road in Fallon County

Cottonwood Creek Bridge is pretty lonely these days, yearning for some traffic to strain its wooden timbers. Under its span trickles the creek of the same name, muddy and high in the spring and barely a flow in the fall. A few scattered and gnarly cottonwood trees dot the dirt banks. Otherwise, the landscape is open and flat all the way to the nearest town of Ismay, 6 miles away. A secondary gravel road, Ismay Road, crosses the bridge.

Since it was built in 1934, it has seen its share of vehicles, from Model Ts to SUVs. Similar bridges dot Montana's countryside, built in response to the emerging car culture of the twenties and thirties. Bridging creeks and gullies stitched communities and far-flung farmsteads together. In its own small way, the timber-stringer bridge helped lay the foundation for what would become Montana's largest industry: agriculture. Bridging barriers like coulees and watercourses may not seem like a historic highlight, but in a state with rugged landscapes, these bridges were huge contributors to economic development, no less so than the mighty railroads. Across Cottonwood Creek Bridge's deck moved every manner of grain truck, farm implement, tractor, and stock truck. In a social sense, it helped move farmhands to fields and families to threshing bees, churches, and schools. All told, there were 1,242 bridges of this style constructed in the state.

Timber-stringer bridges were easy to build, which is one reason why they proliferated. The Montana Highway Department awarded bids to contractors who were obligated to assiduously follow department design specifications. Local farmers and ranchers often bartered their labor in return for having their county bridge taxes waived. Most dimension lumber was gathered from local mills and lumber yards, with Douglas fir being the preferred wood type. The timber bridges of this period could be anywhere from one to forty-two spans, four pilings to a span with wood braces. The wooden decks were covered with gravel or asphalt. Double-coursed wooden guardrails were bolted to the outside stringers.

Emil Prahl and Henry Sawtell, both of Miles City, built Cottonwood Creek Bridge. The bridge has a five-span continuous treated-timber-stringer design, is 95 feet long, and has a 20-foot-wide single lane. At its ends are timber abutments and wingwalls braced with wood pilings. It's a truly functional workhorse.

—PHOTO BY ROB STUTZ, LICENSE CC SA 4.0 INTERNATIONAL (image is not copyrighted as part of this book)

The official NRHP documentation speaks to the historic value of the site:

> The number of timber bridges built on Montana's primary and secondary highways peaked between 1930 and 1935, which coincided with the highway department's increased programs during the Great Depression. While timber bridges were constructed after World War II, their use was limited to secondary highways. Eventually they were supplanted by steel stringer and prestressed concrete structures. Timber bridges, however, still exist in large numbers in eastern Montana and are a testament to the Montana Highway Department's early road-building efforts.

Cottonwood Creek Bridge is one of those survivors. This utilitarian bridge is no beauty queen, but it earned its historic plaque and placement alongside Montana's loftier historic locales.

10

HORNADAY CAMP

46°58′11″N 107°23′58″W

10 miles south of State Highway 200 in Garfield County

In late fall 1886, William T. Hornaday and six other hunters camped in the harsh and unforgiving land of north-central Montana, in what is now Garfield County. The location of their camp is less important than the purpose of their mission. By the late 1880s, the plains buffalo had been nearly exterminated. Hornaday and his colleagues had been dispatched to Montana Territory to obtain suitable specimens for the Smithsonian Institution to display at its museum in Washington, DC. The institution's goal was to acquire samples before the bison became extinct, and the broad expanse of plains and tablelands between the Musselshell and Yellowstone Rivers, where fragments of the last wild herds remained, had been chosen as the collection site.

Hornaday was a natural choice for the expedition. By the time he arrived in Montana at age thirty-one, he was already a world-recognized wildlife author, museum taxidermist, field zoologist, and strong proponent of the wildlife conservation movement of the late 1880s. The timing of the trip—the brutally cold months of November and December—was significant to their success. Bison, the largest mammal in North America, puts on a heavy coat in late fall as winter approaches, and Hornaday and his hunters sought specimens in this prime condition. They harvested twenty-two buffalo from the surrounding coulees and benches at the headwaters of Big Porcupine Creek. Their base camp consisted of a Sibley tent, commonly used by the military during that period, a freight wagon, horses, supplies, a "cook outfit," and baggage. They created a small kitchen dugout against a hillside to escape the persistent winds.

Back in DC, Hornaday created an unorthodox display for the bison. Instead of the usual practice of a placing a single animal on a wooden pedestal, he opted for a family group in a prairie setting. These six buffalo were on prominent display for seventy years. During that time, the large and shaggy bull became a national symbol whose likeness is on the US Department of Interior's great seal and appears on the National Park Service badge. The bison's likeness also appears on coins, stamps, and paper currency. America's infatuation with the bison continues to this day. In 2016 it was designated the nation's national mammal, an honor that would have pleased Hornaday greatly.

In 1955, the group of six was dismantled, returned to Montana, and placed in storage. Following decades of neglect, the mounts underwent complete restoration and found a new place for public display in 1996 at the Museum of the Northern Great Plains in Fort Benton. The final chapter of the Montana bison collected at Hornaday Camp ends, appropriately, back in Montana, where the family group once lived.

—PHOTO BY MICHAEL OBER

—PHOTO BY STEVE WOODRUFF

The actual campsite, at that time a bony, roadless expanse in north-central Montana, is more of a concept than a place. It is where preservation caught up with extinction. There is no visual record of Hornaday's activities there apart from the barely visible kitchen dugout and the sere and lonely landscape. Though Hornaday traveled in Montana on many other occasions, according to the official NRHP wording: "The Hornaday Camp site in Montana is likely the only property remaining that bears a direct and personal association with William T. Hornaday." Nominated to the NRHP in 1991, it is the only nationally designated historic site in Garfield County.

11

FORT ASSINIBOINE

48°29′59″N 109°47′39″W

South of US 87 in Havre, Hill County

Fort Assiniboine was the largest military fort built in Montana during the Indian conflict period of the late nineteenth century. It bested other rival forts in troop size, acreage, and buildings many times over, but it never experienced any military action against "hostile Indians." By the time the original buildings were completed in 1884, Indian conflict had ceased and the native peoples of the northern plains—Métis, Chippewa Cree, Blackfeet, Gros Ventre, and Assiniboine—had melded into varied rhythms of assimilation with white settlers, cattlemen, and townspeople. The fort was an anachronistic throwback to a time that had passed it by.

For a brief period, however, Fort Assiniboine experienced a tenure that earned it the nickname "West Point of the West." Military officers and cavalry personnel trained in the varied landscapes surrounding the nearby Bears Paw Mountains. At peak garrison strength there were more than one thousand soldiers at the fort. Both officers and enlisted soldiers considered the fort a desirable posting because of its elegant brick buildings, commodious housing, and refined atmosphere. Fort Assiniboine boasted a library, a chapel, a hospital, a firing range, a bakery, an exchange store, an underground brick-lined water system, and even a bowling alley. At the center of it all was an enormous parade ground.

When not drilling or on field maneuvers, post officials hosted grand balls and dinner gatherings complete with concerts and exotic menu items freighted in on Great Northern Railway trains from the upper Midwest. In summer months, wagon trains headed to the Bears Paw Mountains for lavish picnics and to escape the heated prairie. The country club atmosphere of the fort aided in cementing a harmonious symbiosis with the nearby community of Havre. The post's colorful band was always a welcome sight in Havre's parades and at social events.

In coming to terms with the end of the Indian conflict period, Congress ordered that Fort Assiniboine be closed, and military activities ceased on May 11, 1911. Its time in history gone, the fort was turned over to the state of Montana in 1916 to be used as an agricultural experiment station, and part of the reserve was set aside as the Rocky Boy's Indian Reservation.

As years went by, some of the smaller buildings burned down or were torn down, their bricks salvaged for homes in nearby Havre or for the construction of Pershing Hall on the campus of Montana State University–Northern. Some post structures were moved to serve as depot buildings or track-repair facilities for the railway. Of the original 104 Fort buildings, only 18 remain today. Many of these are the stately brick officers' quarters that once faced the parade grounds. Throughout the former fort compound are NRHP plaques describing the last moments of the great nineteenth-century Indian conflicts.

—PHOTO BY STEVE WOODRUFF

12

SQUARE BUTTE JAIL

47°31′02″N 110°11′52″W

In the town of Square Butte in Chouteau County

At the edge of Square Butte, on weeded-over Salisbury Street, sits a three-room stone jail that likely hosted more children than desperados. The long-empty Square Butte Jail is a reminder of a time when Montana settlers sought justice to salve perceived ills—even when there weren't any bad guys to be found. If truth is tethered to the facts, inmates for the jail were in short supply just after it was built in 1916, and it never fulfilled its original purpose.

In 1915, the residents of the tiny town of Square Butte complained to the Chouteau County commissioners that their community was "seriously suffering from an oversupply of tramps, beggars and vagabonds." The petitioners felt these individuals threatened peace and endangered lives and thereby demanded a constable, a jail, and a justice of the peace. Their request was granted, and the stone jail was constructed with native rock, in twelve-inch-thick blocks, from nearby quarries. The haphazard arrangement of the blocks suggests that the job was not contracted to a professional mason. The jail has two cells and one entry office. The ceiling and floor are solid concrete, still showing the wood grain of the forms. The steel-barred windows and entry door are still symbolically in place. The wooden window sashes have disappeared, but the original window frames remain.

The backstory of Square Butte Jail is that it was used only as a temporary facility. It was never fully staffed and lacked a passable road connecting it to the county jail in Fort Benton. So realistically, it only served as a holding cell. The jail probably served the community in more practical ways than housing inmates in its early years. A local bachelor and farmer lived in it during the 1930s. County road crews often used it as a bunkhouse. In happier times, "It furnished two or three generations of Square Butte children with a unique clubhouse." During harvest time, local farmers boarded up the windows and used the jail as a temporary granary.

Square Butte never incorporated as a formal town. One of many homesteader and railroad whistle-stops destined for a brief life and hard times, it long ago stopped looking to the future. Today, only the quarried stone jail and schoolhouse remain to look out over the abandoned townsite, whose townspeople were bent on justice but short on evildoers.

—PHOTO BY MICHAEL OBER

13

LEWISTOWN SATELLITE AIRFIELD

47°02′50″N 109°27′30″W

At the municipal airport in Lewistown in Fergus County

The Norden bombsight was one of the best-kept military secrets of World War II. Its technology enabled US Army Air Corps bombers to drop bombs with frightening accuracy from high altitudes. So secret was the Norden that bombardiers were required to take an oath during their training stating that they would defend its secret with their own life. Should an airman fail to protect the device, each bombsight was equipped with a thermite grenade that could melt it and prevent its capture.

According to the NRHP documentation, "the 50-pound bombsight contained over two thousand precision parts—a collection of gyros, motors, gears, mirrors, and levers—that reportedly could 'put bombs in a pickle barrel.'" Still, it was entirely a mechanical device that depended on a navigator's skill in setting and configuring its actions, thus proper training was crucial. The Air Corps searched for locations with clear skies, unlimited open terrain, and remoteness (to aid secrecy) where navigators could test the bombsight, and Lewistown fit the bill.

Today, adjacent to the Lewistown Municipal Airport sits a tiny, unimposing structure in which the Norden bombsight was stored between bombing runs. This structure is part of an NRHP complex that includes a gigantic hangar that housed B-17 bombers. During its World War II use, the airfield boasted enlisted-personnel barracks, dining facilities, sports fields, officers' quarters, and a fuel depot, but it is the storage building—all 173 square feet of it—that makes the complex unique. When in use, it was surrounded by a six-foot-nine, seven-strand barbed-wire fence. Inside, beyond dual wooden weather doors, was a steel vault door with a combination lock. The entire building was constructed of poured concrete. A small guard post flanked the fence gate. It was the only building at the airport kept under twenty-four-hour guard. After each training run, the bombsight was carefully removed from a B-17 and returned, under guard, by specially trained security airmen. Similar storage buildings popped up at training bases all over the nation during the war, but, according to the US Air Force, the one in Lewistown is the only one still standing.

So it was, for a while, that the skies over Montana were filled with lumbering B-17s and the infamous Norden bombsight. Such training in strategic bombing, new to warfare in the 1940s, had good results. The NHRP nomination document states: "The Montana-trained squadrons flew a total of 1,263 combat missions, dropped 71,128 tons of bombs, lost 548 aircraft, and shot down 1,018 enemy aircraft without ever turning away from a mission."

The training center was active for only one year, from November 1942 until late 1943. In February 1947, the military gave it to the city of Lewistown and Fergus County, and a municipal airport has occupied the facility ever since. The hulking hangar, sturdy bombsight storage facility, and a few outbuildings harken back to a time when Lewistown and Montana's endless skies made their contribution to the war effort.

The old hangar, now used for the municipal airport. —PHOTO BY FRED IHDE

The cement storage facility. —PHOTO BY MICHAEL OBER

14
DEAN SCHOOL

45°24′16″N 109°41′24″W

1367 Nye Road in Stillwater County

Against narrow odds, Montana still has numerous operational one-room schools. At one time, there were more than 2,500 of them scattered across Montana's vast and varied landscape. Now they number fewer than fifty. The Dean School, in Stillwater County, stands on an acre of land donated by a local landowner in 1915, a practice not uncommon in early times, before formal school districts could be organized and funded. Though now a community center, the Dean School educated generations of Montana's rural kids.

One-room schools revolved around the rhythms and demands of rural livelihoods. Teachers were often itinerant, moving from one district to another, or were local women pressed into service. Some boarded with nearby families. Most rural schools went only to grade eight, because young boys and girls were needed back on the farm or ranch to fulfill their roles as the next generation of agricultural producers. Some students, though, transferred to towns and made their way through the local high school and beyond.

Days began with the raising of the American flag, the recitation of the Pledge of Allegiance, and the singing of "God Bless America." Then there were lessons in Palmer penmanship and the basics of letters, numbers, civics, geography, and history. Afternoons were structured around story readings by the teacher and older students. At recess, there were fox and geese games, footraces, and pump, pump, pull away. At Dean School, the boys often dammed Meadow Creek to form an ice-skating pond.

The multigrade Dean School answered the challenge of teaching different skill levels and ages. Older students served as coteachers and mentors in a collaborative system. Similarly, neighbors and family members pitched in by using their freight wagons to haul firewood and coal, the latter of which was abundant in Stillwater County's exposed seams and mines, and hay to feed to the children's horses, which they rode to school from their homes. A garage and storage shed, still standing, kept everything dry. At day's end, students hauled water, swept floors, and cleaned the blackboard, which is still in place.

A teacherage, attached to the schoolhouse, provided spartan accommodations for the teacher. It now functions as a small community kitchen. Above the schoolhouse's front entrance hangs a sign that proudly proclaims its lengthy rural history: "Dean School 1914–1967." The turreted and louvered bell tower, with the original bell, hangs in the sheltered main entry. The solid maple floor, worn shiny by little feet, stretches edge to edge in the central room. Telltale burn marks reveal where the large potbellied stove once stood. Above, the pressed-tin ceiling, now painted white, stares down

—PHOTO © CHARLOTTE CALDWELL, www.CharlotteCaldwell.com

on the room where young children moved through the grades and marched on to adulthood. Ringing the room, under the long bank of windows, are hooks that held student's clothes, lunch bags, hats, and mittens. Two outhouses were replaced by boys' and girls' bathrooms built into the front entryway, the only significant architectural change to the original footprint. In all, the building is what one might picture when envisioning the quintessential rural one-room schoolhouse.

15

ROOSEVELT ARCH

45°00'24"N 110°41'58"W

Entrance to Yellowstone National Park at Gardiner in Park County

From a distance, starkly alone amid an unfettered landscape, the towering stone monolith of Roosevelt Arch looks impossibly out of place, though it has greeted countless millions of park visitors since stonemasons finished it in 1903. The North Entrance Check Station is the official entry point to Yellowstone National Park at Gardiner, but the 50-foot-tall Roosevelt Arch is the symbolic entrance. Before the park's road was rerouted to accommodate long lines of traffic, the arch was much closer to the entrance station.

Two stone towers hold up the curved archway 30 feet above the ground, forming the portal. Huge blocks of basalt, quarried nearby, were used to construct the arch, giving it a natural and weathered look. Little in the way of finished pointing can be found at the stone joints, giving the whole edifice a rugged and enduring appeal. Sloped wing walls of matching basalt, terminated with matching stone turrets, flank the arch. Theodore Roosevelt, for whom the arch is named, was present at the dedication ceremony in 1903. Above the north-facing arch is the inscription "For the Benefit and Enjoyment of the People," an extract from the Organic Act creating the Park and bearing upon the conservation work of Theodore Roosevelt.

The arch itself is part of the larger North Entrance Road Historic District, which includes the challenging 5-mile-long road to Mammoth Hot Springs that flanks the Gardner River and passes through a narrow canyon. Historic features along the way, including culverts, stone flumes, headwalls, and guard walls, highlight the engineering, construction, and design that went into this historic park road. They have changed little over time. In 2002, the arch was listed on the NRHP, in honor of the years it has welcomed park visitors, from those who arrived in horse-drawn surreys to those in sleek and modern automobiles.

—PHOTO BY MICHAEL OBER

—PHOTO BY MICHAEL OBER

16

EAGLE GUARD STATION

46°19′15″N 111°42′26″W

11 miles west of Townsend in Broadwater County

In 1895, gold miner Dick Owen built a one-story log structure as a home for him and his wife, Sarah, and their daughter, Sadie, west of what is now Townsend. As local mines played out, the Owen family moved to nearby Radersburg to operate a boardinghouse, abandoning the cabin. When the Helena National Forest was created in 1908, it acquired the rundown homestead and repaired it for administrative use, calling it Eagle Guard Station. Just about every one of Montana's seven national forests has such a remote outpost cabin.

From 1908 until the early 1950s, the cabin housed trail crews, smoke chasers, and forest rangers, chiefly on a seasonal basis. After that, it was made available, on a lease basis, to local range riders and cattle hands from the Crow and Indian Creek Livestock Association. On-again, off-again occupancy contributed to its structural decline over the next three decades, until the Helena National Forest decided to rehabilitate it and place it into its cabin rental program (see Wurtz Homestead and Gird Point Lookout).

Between 1991 and 1994, US Forest Service personnel and volunteers restored the cabin using primitive building skills and donated materials. The current NRHP site consists of the cabin, a woodshed, a toilet, a barn, horse corrals, and a fire ring. Added to the NRHP in 2001, Eagle Guard Station is the oldest administrative log structure on the Helena National Forest. It serves as a rustic reminder of the early days of the US Forest Service.

—PHOTO BY US FOREST SERVICE

—PHOTO BY US FOREST SERVICE

17

MONTANA STATE TRAINING SCHOOL

46°13′52″N 112°08′24″W

Off State Highway 281 in Boulder in Jefferson County

In 1887, during Montana's late territorial period, Governor Preston Leslie requested that the federal government provide the territory with an institution for the "deaf and dumb." Funds were never appropriated, but Congress offered public land instead, which Montana had in abundance. When Montana gained statehood in 1889, the state sold 50,000 acres to raise funds for the asylum, or the Montana State Training School as it was named. However, due to tight budgets, the asylum wasn't funded until 1893, when the legislature selected the town of Boulder as its site.

Prominent Montana architect John C. Paulsen designed the main building at the training school, as well as several of Montana's other notable buildings of the late nineteenth century, including the Broadwater Hotel, Helena High School, and the first Montana Club, all of which have since been destroyed. In addition to the asylum, major Paulsen buildings remaining from that period include the "Main Halls" at Montana State University, University Montana Western, and Montana Tech, and the Jefferson County Courthouse in Boulder. Paulson chose an Italianate superstructure made with local brick to house the training school. He combined a base layer of locally sourced granite and trimmed it with what is said to be Montana copper.

In 1903 the institution became the Montana School for the Deaf and Dumb, though the prominent letters that frame the arched main entrance still read "Montana State Training School." The first mentally handicapped youths were admitted to the school in that year as well, and their numbers grew for several years. By the 1930s, nearly all of the residents at the school suffered from mental illnesses rather than speech and hearing disorders. In 1937 the "deaf and dumb" training programs for speech and hearing disorders were transferred to Great Falls.

Today the school's halls and classrooms are silent, which is fitting, because for many years silence was the rule for the youthful residents. The roof leaks, the gutter system has largely collapsed, water stains mark some interior walls, many windows are boarded up, and the brick and mortar have succumbed to the elements. Nonetheless, Paulson's impressive structure survives. It serves as the storage facility and central landmark of the Boulder River School and Hospital. Surrounded by an apron of green grass and mature trees, silence and muted tones seem to have a forever grip on the structure.

—PHOTO BY MICHAEL OBER

18

GIRD POINT LOOKOUT

46°12'27"N 113°54'42"W

North of Skalkaho Road in the Sapphire Mountains in Ravalli County

Built in 1939, Gird Point Lookout sits atop a rocky outcrop east of Hamilton. There, nestled in a grandiose panorama of the Sapphire Mountains, sits this piece of Montana's forest history. To get there one follows a rugged fifteen-mile-long one-lane road, tracing a line back in time.

In the years following the famous 1910 fires that scorched millions of acres in Idaho and Montana, federal and state forest managers determined that fire detection and suppression required a rigorous network of fire lookouts. What emerged from their epiphany was a building boom between 1920 and 1945. Lookouts of various designs were built; some sat on tall stilts, some were merely small one-room boxes on the ground, but all were located on strategic mountaintops and staffed by trained observers and smoke chasers.

In 1984, Gird Point and seven other unstaffed lookouts were scheduled to be torn down, having been eclipsed by better technology. Early detection no longer depended upon people on peaks. Fixed-wing aircraft (even drones), helicopters, and satellites are better tools for locating remote fires today. Gird Point's story was the same for lookouts all across the West.

But fire lookout lore runs deep and strong in Montana. Active citizens and organizations have partnered with land-management agencies to keep these mountaintop structures alive. While most have been removed, a few have survived as both staffed and unstaffed points of interest. Many have been placed on the NRHP, including Gird Point in 2002, in honor of their service of safeguarding forests and rangeland. The Bitterroot National Forest manages Gird Point as one of its three rental lookouts, available to the public. The Forest Service now operates twenty-one restored fire lookouts in its rental program in Montana.

The lookout itself was built in a standard design using prefab dimension lumber sawn in Spokane, Washington, and trucked and packed to the site. Local timber supports elevate the 14-foot-by-14-foot "live-in-cab" building 8 feet above ground. Swing-out shutters flank the wraparound windows and fold in for winter security, and the structure is surrounded with a 360-degree catwalk. Inside, following a standard layout, are wooden bed frames with storage bunkers underneath, a small kitchen work surface, a stove, chairs, a desk, and a small refrigerator. At the center is the dependable Osborne fire finder, still functional after eight decades of use. The floor plan is not unlike almost all the surviving fire lookouts still in use today. Little has changed, to the delight of fire lookout buffs everywhere.

—PHOTO BY STEVE WOODRUFF

19

ALTA RANGER STATION

45°37′08″N 114°17′55″W

South of Connor in Ravalli County

In the far-off reaches of the southern Bitterroot Mountains is a small one-room, dirt-floored log cabin, humble in appearance but of outsized historic proportions. Revered by some in the US Forest Service culture as a holy grail in their agency's lore, the Alta Ranger Station stands proudly as the first ranger station in the United States.

Alta has a quirky origins story. Prior to there being a US Forest Service, public lands were administered by the General Land Office of the Interior Department. In Montana, the Bitterroot Forest Reserve was established in 1897, and two forest rangers, Nathaniel Wilkerson and Henry Tuttle, were assigned the task of patrolling the West Fork of the Bitterroot River, apprehending timber poachers and illegal grazers. Accordingly, they built a small one-room log cabin on Hughes Creek to serve as a ranger post. Using a borrowed mule, they skidded their own logs and spent their own money to purchase other building materials. They officially dedicated it on July 4, 1899. Later, it was discovered that the cabin was on a miner's private claim, and the General Land Office abandoned it in 1904. And there it sat for thirty-seven years.

Recognizing the cabin's significance, the Hamilton Lion's Club purchased it from the daughter of the miner in 1941 and then donated it to the US Forest Service, which set about restoring it to period-perfect 1899 authenticity. In 1941, 1952, and 1974 it received some stabilization efforts, but no focused professional preservation. Nonetheless, over the ensuing years, Alta enjoyed several additional restoration periods as US Forest Service crews and volunteers replaced windows, door frames, the sod roof, and sill logs, and repaired drainage elevations, all efforts aimed at stabilizing the cabin as a nonfunctional museum piece. The ranger station celebrated its one-hundredth anniversary in 1999. Neighbors, visitors, and Forest Service dignitaries partook of an old-fashioned cake-and-lemonade picnic under a vintage forty-five-star American flag. Though documentation is difficult, it is likely the oldest surviving building associated with federal forest management.

In recent years, when forest fires erupt in the southern Bitterroot National Forest, wildland fire crews lovingly wrap the cabin with fireproof foil coverings. Just in case. When the threat has passed, the coveted assignment of unwrapping the cabin and raising the American flag over it is offered to select hotshot crews or smokejumpers who request the honor. Each time it emerges, fiercely proud of its legacy.

—PHOTO BY MICHAEL OBER

20

SAVENAC NURSERY

47°23′07″N 115°23′47″W

Along I-90 south of Haugen in Mineral County

When Elers Koch established a small nursery on the Lolo National Forest in 1907, he likely didn't know that it would last for sixty-two years and figure mightily in the nation's reforestation efforts. It was the first of its kind and grew to be the largest and oldest operating tree nursery within the US Forest Service. From its base in Haugen, native rootstock seedlings were shipped all over the western United States. The story of the Savenac Nursery joins together four themes of historic proportions that greatly impacted western forestlands: the Great Burn of 1910, Koch's legacy, the birth of professional forestry, and the Civilian Conservation Corps.

Koch was a man of many firsts. He was the first supervisor of the Lolo and Bitterroot National Forests, a groundbreaking silviculturalist, a pioneering forest manager, and a leader in developing wildland firefighting techniques and skills in the early years of the Forest Service. He was one of the first graduates of the Yale School of Forestry (1902) and one of the country's first professional foresters. At a time when most foresters in the West were from the East, he was a native Montanan. He was also one of the first foresters to use writing skills and scholarly publications to promote conservation and wise reforestation practices following logging and wildfire. He was also an outdoorsman of renown throughout Montana, and he and two others are credited with the first ascent of Granite Peak in 1923, Montana's highest mountain at 12,799 feet.

In an age when industrial-scale tree harvesting and timber poaching on public lands were rampant, he saw the need to cultivate new stock for ravished woodlands. For his nursery site Koch looked west of Missoula to the abandoned homestead of a German settler named Savennach. A key factor in the site decision was its location along the historic Mullan Road. The Milwaukee Railroad, completed over the divide along the Montana-Idaho border in 1909, finalized the transportation link that allowed the nursery to ship seedlings throughout the West. Eventually the Mullan Road became US 10 (and now I-90), expanding the travel routes to and from the nursery compound.

Ironically, just three years after the creation of the nursery, it burned down in the historic forest fire of 1910, known as the Great Burn. While Koch was directing firefighting crews nearby, the nursery was lost, along with 3 million acres of old-growth timber and several nearby towns, including Avery and Wallace, Idaho, and Haugen, Taft, Saltese, and De Borgia, Montana. Every building at Savenac was destroyed, but the sprawling seedbeds survived because the irrigation system kept them cool and moist. The fire-devastated forestlands underscored the need for replacement trees. Forest Service

—PHOTO BY STEVE WOODRUFF

personnel responded with a spirited rebuilding campaign and were soon cultivating acres of ponderosa pine, Engelmann spruce, Douglas fir, and western white pine seedlings.

In the 1930s the trained labor force of the Civilian Conservation Corps (CCC) expanded Savenac on a large scale. Beginning in 1936, the boys of the CCC company 956 began to construct buildings and other structures that define the site and last to this day. Nursery crews constructed cone sheds, transplant plots, irrigation and pumping systems, seed storage and packaging barns, and even a visitor facility for a growing number of curious tourists and guests. At the nursery's peak, two hundred men working the vast seedbeds and transplant plots boosted production to twelve million seedlings per year. The nursery closed in 1969.

Today's visitors and history buffs can still find evidence of these former times. Examples include abandoned telephone poles, the remains of the old Mullan Road, irrigation ditches and roadbeds, an abandoned Pelton wheel used to generate electricity, the former water lagoon, a quintessential stone bridge and entry gate of CCC design, the overgrown remains of curbs and building foundations, an abandoned root cellar, and the original flagpole site. The Savenac Nursery was formally listed on the NRHP in 1999. Elers Koch would be proud to know that elements of his tree farm survive.

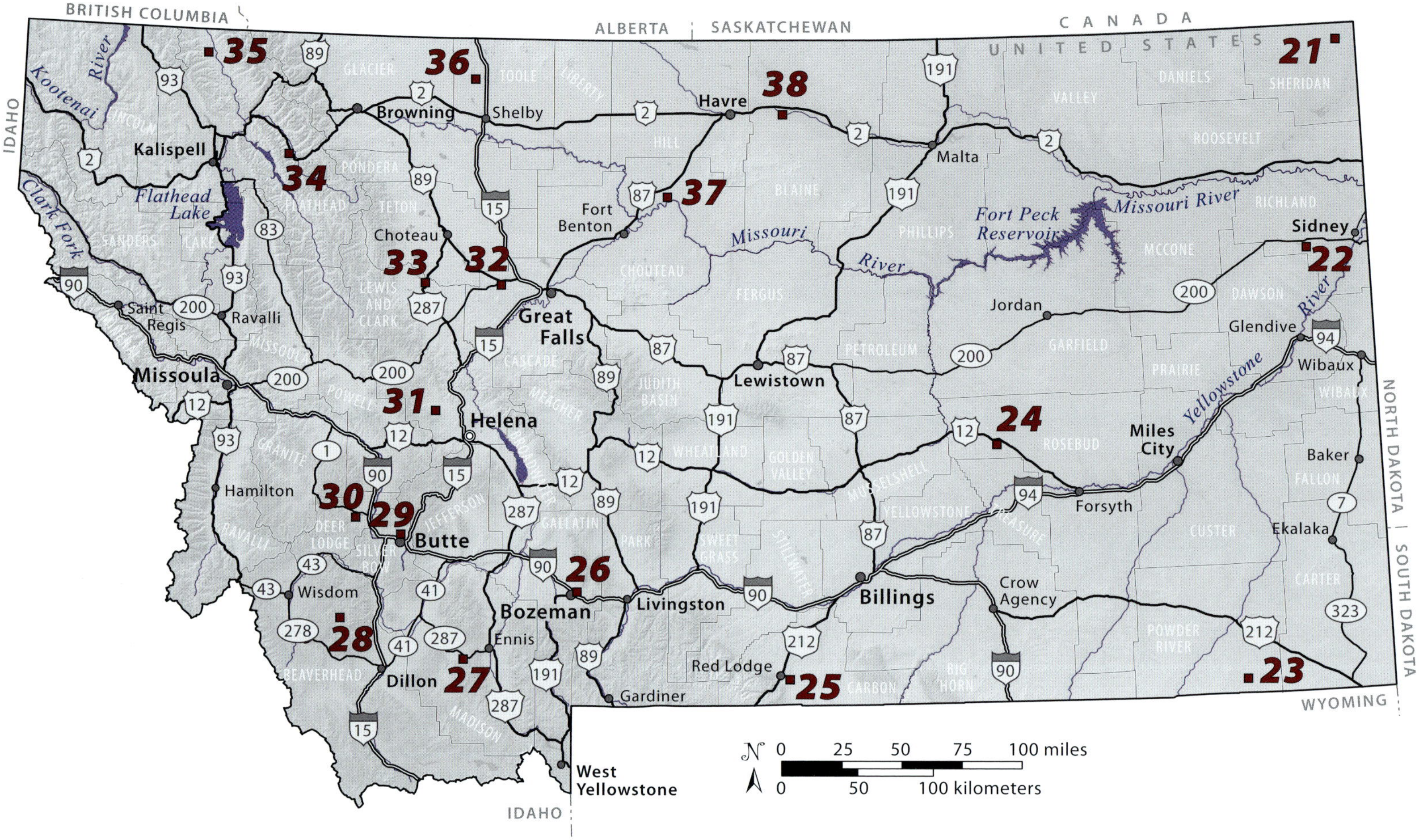

21 Comertown
22 Burgess Garage
23 Cross Ranch Headquarters
24 Jersey Lilly Saloon
25 Smith Mine District
26 Northern Pacific–Story Mill
27 Virginia City
28 Elkhorn-Coolidge Ghost Town
29 Butte-Anaconda Historic District
30 Anaconda Smokestack
31 Methodist-Episcopal Church of Marysville
32 J. C. Adams Stone Barn
33 Gilman State Bank
34 Izaak Walton Inn
35 Wurtz Homestead
36 Kevin Depot
37 Virgelle Mercantile and Bank
38 Dave's Texaco

The Business of Settlement

Other than the discovery of gold in 1862, there was little to support Montana's bid to become a territory—much less a state—in the mid-nineteenth century. Abraham Lincoln, his administration, and Congress back east, busy managing the Civil War, saw little to gain by adding to the United States a new territory in the faraway West. Montana had no court system or justices, no volunteer militia, no emerging industry or economy, no transportation network, and no stable settlements beyond some scattered hardscrabble mining "gulch towns." It was gold, which Lincoln needed badly to fund the war, and the opportunity to draw in a slave-free territory to the Union that tipped the decision to establish Montana as a territory in 1864. Twenty-five years would pass before Congress acknowledged Montana's petition for statehood, finally approved in 1889.

As states developed in accordance with conventional expansionist themes, people typically headed to the hinterlands to clear forests, build homes and small towns, and till the land. They gathered their bounty from the soil and became what Thomas Jefferson termed "sturdy yeoman farmers." With time, economies diversified. Industries followed the plow, and the workforce shifted from growing things to making things. Factories displaced farmlands, and heavy industry and transportation routes gained supremacy.

In Montana, things happened in reverse order. Montana was industrial before it became agricultural. Today, the state's number-one industry is agriculture. But in the booming late nineteenth century, Montana was a raw and visceral place, marked in corresponding ways by the smell, noise, bustle, and surge of heavy industry. Two things drove its industrial development: the arrival of the railroad in the 1880s and the relentless pursuit of natural resources. Before homesteaders swept into Montana in the early 1900s and broke the soil for farm crops, nearly a generation of laborers had already been hard at digging up coal, silver, gold, and copper from the land and processing it in gigantic smelters and mills. Other industries, such as timber cutting and milling and railroad construction, complemented this industrial and settlement period.

The slow and inexorable transition from territory to statehood and beyond left tracings of the physical settlement along the way. When it comes to historic Montana sites, there's a treasure trove of places left over from this industrial period, including mining camps, railroad depots, barns, and smokestacks.

21
COMERTOWN

48°53′49″N 104°15′00″W

West of Westby in Sheridan County

Native shrubs and persistent prairie grass have all but reclaimed the former community of Comertown. Here and there a lilac bush or a Russian olive mingles with a crumbled foundation and evidence of human landscaping: a collapsed fence, rusted pipes, tin canisters. Random two-track dirt lanes mark the former streets. An empty rail passenger car tilts lazily to the side, its trucks removed. It recalls the days when the Soo Line bravely extended its steel rails to Plentywood and Westby, hoping to extract from the stubborn plains grain grown by equally stubborn homesteaders. Across it all, and under the broad vault of sky that often held more betrayal than hope for farmers, blow the endless winds of the rolling flatlands.

In northeast Montana such tiny pioneer towns—Flaxville, Dooley, Westby, Raymond, Outlook, Redstone—were commonplace. Each hoped to advance in prosperity and perhaps ascend to become the seat of Sheridan County. Plentywood emerged as the seat of county government in 1913, and the other nearby towns began to fade away, including Comertown, which is no longer listed on Montana highway maps.

In its best of times there was a café, two general stores, a carefully landscaped town park, a cemetery, two lumber yards, two grain elevators, and two bars. Through the frenzied period of the homestead era, towns competed fiercely with each other for people and economic status. There were four fundamental elements needed to compose a "town" in Montana: bank, school, post office, and railroad. Comertown had an elementary school, a post office, and a branch rail line, but little else. While the elementary school caused many farmers to establish small residences in the town so their children could go to school in the winter months, there was never a vibrant commercial sector, especially after most of the retail businesses burned down in the early 1920s. Valiantly, a Works Progress Administration project in the 1930s created a dormitory-style high school, home of the Comertown Coyotes, hoping to draw farm kids to town. It was the last roll of the dice to try and secure Comertown's future.

By the 1950s, though, with the departure of many homesteaders, Westby and Plentywood became the focal points for commercial and social activity for the folks who remained. Soo Line service to the area ended, and the post office closed. Comertown's meager retail district imploded as a result. Due to extensive enrollment declines, the high school closed in 1953, the grade school in 1965. The grade school's closing was the death knell for Comertown,

—PHOTO BY MARVEL HELLEGAARD

as it had been its final reason for existence. By the 1970s the town was abandoned, part of history's backwash.

Comertown was placed on the NRHP in 1993. The official NRHP plaque looks out over the former townsite as if presiding over a cemetery. Boom-and-bust towns are not atypical in Montana, and Comertown tells the tale of numerous similar places, where dreams of permanency and solvency tried to take root—and failed.

22

BURGESS GARAGE

47°41'06"N 104°37'15"W

In Lambert in Richland County

At the corner of Third and Main in Lambert sits the Burgess Garage, a very unprepossessing structure with a flat roof and squatty appearance. Though it possesses little in the way of architectural splendor, the garage was a bedrock business in a prime location: corner lot facing Main Street in a hopeful town.

The Burgess Garage was constructed sometime around 1913, at the dawn of the motorcar and mechanized farm machinery era. Where there had once been more of a need for livery stables and harness makers in Lambert, the spread of the automobile sparked the need for skilled mechanics and machinists—and garages. The Burgess Garage serviced the locals' passenger cars and trucks, and also sold and maintained agricultural equipment. The building housed a commercial garage throughout its entire period of operation, but other businesses were sometimes located inside it in quirky arrangements. For a time, it served as the office of the town's only doctor, and for a few years the owner/editor of the town's newspaper, the *Lambert Promoter*, operated out of an office in the garage too. The structure is a testament to the resourcefulness of remote towns bent on finding solutions to local challenges.

As a homesteaders' headquarters, fueled by the Enlarged Homestead Act of 1909, Lambert's fortunes rose and fell with the times. Prior to the collapse of the homestead era, the town, according to the NRHP documents, had "three lumberyards, three livery and feed stables, two dance halls, four grocers, two pool halls, two barbershops with five barbers, two hotels, six cafes, a dray line (shipping), three garages, two oil companies, four saloons, two bowling alleys, a drugstore, several dry-goods and hardware stores, a phone company, and a post office." Tragically, a series of fires (1921, 1925, and 1931) wiped out the business district of Lambert so that nothing is left of the original fifty-two commercial outlets except the Burgess Garage. Though vacant for years, it stands at the center of Lambert, and the small but resolute community nominated the Burgess Garage to the NRHP in 2004 to honor the town's heritage.

In sum, there is little that's remarkable about the Burgess Garage. There is no dramatic storyline here. It was a mechanic's garage. Its deeper story, however, lies in the history of the small town around it, and the times in which it developed. When measured against Montana's more well-established communities, Lambert comes up short with diminished dimensions. But sites like this garage, found in many of Montana's unremembered towns, are achingly relevant to Montana's broader story. They are the mileposts of Montana history.

—PHOTO BY MELISSA MARKWORDT

23

CROSS RANCH HEADQUARTERS

45°05′44″N 105°19′10″W

East of State Highway 59 about 26 miles south of Broadas in Powder River County

On the way to just about nowhere sits a cluster of three weathered buildings near Biddle, Montana. They are the remaining headquarters of the Cross Ranch, a sprawling cattle kingdom of the kind that was once common to southeast Montana. Most human enterprises were poorly matched for this tortured and arid stretch of land, unless you were a cattleman. The original owner was Spencer Fullerton Baird Biddle, born to a wealthy Philadelphia family. In 1885 Biddle staked a claim to cattle holdings that sat astride the old Texas Trail, from which millions of longhorns poured onto Montana's vast free-grazing prairies.

Biddle witnessed the awful winter of 1886–87, when the open-range cattle industry collapsed and numerous ranch operations went bankrupt and were sold at auction. But fortune smiles on those who plan. With no small measure of luck and entrepreneurialism, Biddle doubled down, bought some nearby grazing land, imported Scottish Highlander breeds, and prospered. The minimalist strategies of the old open range gave way to today's more defined grazing districts, fenced range, diversified and hardier breeds, and supplemental haying and feeding tactics, but operations like the Cross Ranch were foundational to today's ranching.

The three main buildings that still survive were built in 1893. The former cookhouse and bunkhouse are of one-story log construction. Inside the log walls, cowpunchers and line riders mended tack and talked the talk of cattlemen: calving, roundups, beef prices, breeds, and brands. The main lodge is a two-story log home built for Biddle and his wife. Neighbors referred to it as the White House because of its white-painted exterior and its large size compared to typical log structures of the prairie, which were low, squatty, and colorless. The wraparound porch added a grace and elegance not seen before in Powder River country.

Historians who wrote the story of the ranch for the NRHP stated, "The headquarters he built . . . might not have been as elaborate if he had not been trying to convince his wife to share what he had found in Montana." His wife, Molly, favored Paris, however, and that is where Biddle finally died in 1929. The main lodge, with its French colonial design, reveals his attempt to make their home a worthy and dignified dwelling amid the harsh surroundings. Though he tried to make her comfortable, she was never enthusiastic about cattle ranching.

Biddle and his wife spent most of their winters away from Montana, traveling the world. Unlike many wealthy and foreign ranch owners, though, Biddle was an engaged livestock producer, spending thirty-four years as owner and manager. He was a charter member of the powerful 1885 Montana Stockgrowers Association and served in the territorial legislature. He spent three decades improving his holdings and breeds between visits to Paris and Philadelphia. He was a kingpin in the industry.

The lodge. —PHOTO BY HOLLY RUMPF

The bunkhouse. —PHOTO BY HOLLY RUMPF

The former headquarters used to sit adjacent to the cottonwood-lined Little Powder River, which watered the cowboys, their horses, and the cattle. In a burst of exuberance, the anemic river meandered a half mile away one spring. The current owners still utilize the main lodge as housing for guided hunting trips, having made only modest modifications to its original layout and decor. Cross Ranch became an NRHP site in 1996, and it is a worthy place to remember what used to be and to reflect upon the remoteness of the early Montana livestock period.

24

JERSEY LILLY SALOON

46°34′39″N 107°22′24″W

In Ingomar in Rosebud County

Montana has no shortage of historic watering holes. They range from the local—and maybe the only—tavern to restored pool halls to craft brewpubs in converted storefronts. Some are relatively famous, such as the Atlas Bar in Columbus, with its built-in spittoons in the foot bar, and the Montana Bar in Miles City, with its cowhide-covered booth seats—both listed on the NRHP. And every town seems to have a favorite, even if it is the only such business in town, like the Jersey Lilly Saloon in Ingomar. To get to this bar (closed at the time of this writing) requires some serious drive time on US 12.

Nominated to the NRHP in 1994, the Jersey Lilly is actually in the building that served as the Wiley, Clark, and Greening Bank (indeed, this is the official NRHP listing), built in October 1914 as the emerging town's first brick structure. Around the bank the town grew amid the frenzy of the homestead era. Then the Milwaukee Railroad came through, bringing more residents with it. Soon there were forty-six businesses, and the town became a major shipping point for sheep and wool. The railroad, bankrupt one year and flush with new investors the next, could never compete with the Great Northern to the north and the Northern Pacific to the south. Its route through central Montana faced innumerable maintenance challenges and management uncertainties. Shipping contracts rose and fell; seasonal businesses resulted in unpredictable profits. Eventually the railroad closed its operations in Montana, and towns like Ingomar began to disappear. The only actual commercial business left in Ingomar today is the Jersey Lilly Saloon that opened in the 1930s. The bank building was made to look more "saloonish" with a rough-hewn awning.

The bar is named after Judge Roy Bean's famous bar in Langtry, Texas. It claims to be the only bar and restaurant in Montana to have outdoor his and hers privies. The cherrywood backbar was one of two that were transported from St. Louis up the Missouri and Yellowstone Rivers to Forsyth in the early 1900s. There it remained in "quarantine" until Prohibition was repealed in 1933. It finally arrived in Ingomar in the back of a Model T and was installed in what was then the Oasis Bar. Through the ensuing years and succession of owners, the bar witnessed the emptying out of the small town as businesses closed, residents moved, and the school shut down. For motorists along US 12, the Jersey Lilly is a reminder that the leftovers of history are often found in the most remote places.

—PHOTO BY MICHAEL OBER

—PHOTO BY MICHAEL OBER

25

SMITH MINE DISTRICT

45°09′25″N 109°10′58″W

Off State Highway 308 near Bear Creek in Carbon County

More than 60 million years ago the organic plant material that would become the vast coal deposits in Carbon County was laid out in a broad subtropical coastal plain. The material was compressed, buried under mud, heated, and converted to peat. Over millions of years, the increased pressure and temperature from burial compressed and baked the peat into high-grade subbituminous coal that, in modern times, became known as the Bear Creek Field.

Among the numerous coal-mining operations to emerge in southeast Montana to harvest this prehistoric fuel was the Smith Mine. Beginning in 1906 and continuing through World War II, the Smith Mine burrowed into this coalfield, supplying fuel to steam-powered railroads and countless homeowners and businesses through two world wars.

Smith Mine is known chiefly for the tragic disaster of the morning of February 27, 1943. Multiple shifts were engaged in meeting the nation's need for wartime coal, and the hillside bustled with round-the-clock activity. Seventy-seven men entered the mine that morning, and only three emerged. According to historians who nominated the site to the NRHP in 2009:

> At 9:37 a.m., an underground explosion and hurricane force winds blowing out of the Number 3 adit signaled that something terrible had happened underground . . . Unfortunately, all rescue efforts failed and one man died as a result of his rescue attempts. Investigations later indicated that thirty miners probably died instantly in the explosion. Carbon monoxide gas and lack of oxygen killed the remaining forty-four men. Five of these men survived for an hour and a half after the explosion, barricaded in a small shop.

Today, there is little evidence of the Bear Creek Field's coal-mining heritage—except for the thirty-four scattered and abandoned buildings at the Smith Mine site. The years have not been kind to them. The dilapidated and crumbling buildings still cling to the hillside, overgrown with prairie grass and sagebrush. Where once industry clanged and hummed on the hillside, now only the muted murmurs of wind can be heard blowing through empty window frames.

26

NORTHERN PACIFIC–STORY MILL HISTORIC DISTRICT

45°41′30″N 111°01′16″W

North of I-90 near L Street in Bozeman in Gallatin County

John Bozeman may have had the city of Bozeman named for him, but it was Nelson Story who guided the town through its infancy and into industrial, transportation, and agricultural preeminence. In so many ways the Northern Pacific–Story Mill Historic District, comprising sixty acres and fifty buildings in northeast Bozeman, enshrines his influence, which extended well beyond the Gallatin Valley.

John Bozeman and Nelson Story were contemporaries, both arriving in the Gallatin Valley in the early 1860s. Bozeman met his end shortly after establishing a tent-and-log-cabin settlement where the valley opens up west of Bozeman Pass. He was gunned down on the Yellowstone River in 1867 either by Blackfeet Indians or by his travel companion, Tom Cover—nobody knows for sure.

Nelson Story had better luck in his search for riches. In 1866 he brought the first cattle drive of Texas longhorns to Montana to feed the gold miners. He took note of the broad Gallatin Valley and its fertile soil, watered by a network of streams, and, eager to establish a business empire, constructed one of the first flour mills there. He capitalized on the labors of settlers and farmers who brought in bountiful yields of oats, sweet peas, flax, wheat, and other grain crops. The military established Fort Ellis nearby, and Story, just the man to cash in on opportunity, sought out lucrative government contracts to provide supplies to the fort.

He could be generous in broad measure but ruthless, cunning, and stubborn in the balance. He crushed competitors with little conscience and proudly bore the reputation as the fierce mogul of his empire. He could be violent, deceitful, and, according to John Russell in *Treasure State Tycoon: Nelson Story and the Making of Montana*, "not at all out of step with dishonesty." Story and his family members expanded their business interests to include freighting, banking, real estate, additional flour mills, mercantile outlets, and rail transport contracts. The late nineteenth century was time of fast fortunes in Montana, and Nelson Story was at the center of it all.

Story built a grandiose home for his family on Bozeman's main street at the time, which was just dirt or mud, depending on the season. From his house, which had the area's first indoor plumbing, doorbell, and brick chimney, he watched Bozeman grow up around him and his entrepreneurial efforts.

MONTANA
CERETANA F
"IT'S THE W

—PHOTOS BY MICHAEL OBER

His mark is everywhere in Bozeman: he was one of the town's first mayors; he donated land in south Bozeman for the creation of Agricultural College, now Montana State University; and Story Street is named for him.

Along the now-abandoned railroad spur corridor that defines the historic district was a variety of utilitarian structures connecting Story's grain mill and other corresponding industrial outlets. These included freight docks and warehouses, a scale house, a water tower, a passenger depot, a coaling dock and roundhouse, oil sheds, stockyards, water canals, and grain elevators. There remains a "domestic trash dump" with archeological potential. Some of the district's assets have been reclaimed and brought to new life, serving as retail and commercial spaces that highlight each building's history. Others have merely moldered and been festooned with "tagger" artwork, leaving pigeons as their only occupants. Community parks and trails have replaced some of the old rail beds.

Though Story died in 1926, his story endures, as captured in the NRHP's 1996 nominating narrative. The Northern Pacific–Story Mill Historic District is

> a well-preserved example of a historic center of transportation and commerce. . . . The district's physical remnants are clearly reflective of the intimate association between railroading and economic development in the Bozeman vicinity, as well as the pronounced local influence of the Nelson Story family. Ultimately, the visual appearance of the district conveys the significant influence of rail systems in shaping Montana's geographic and architectural character.

27

VIRGINIA CITY

45°17′27″N 111°56′35″W

On State Highway 287 in Madison County

History has a way of rubbing up against contemporary life in curious ways. Virginia City is a perfect example of this phenomenon. It has suffered a fate similar to countless other mining towns: boom, depression, abandonment, and a peculiar sort of afterlife. It is a ghost town, a livable community, a county seat (Madison County), a tourist mecca, and an all-around living history museum. If there was a holy grail of Montana historic towns—with a strong nod to Butte—Virginia City would be it. It is Montana's quintessential pioneer town.

Virginia City was once part of a 12-mile-long collection of gold rush camps scattered up and down Alder Gulch. The site became an overnight gold rush mecca in 1863 and became the second Montana territorial capitol in 1865. The region eventually yielded more than 40 million dollars in gold. Along with Bannack, 90 miles away, the town was the epicenter of the infamous Montana vigilante movement that rid the territory of thieves and murderers. It's believed that the population of Virginia City once swelled to nearly ten thousand occupants. Today, there are only two hundred year-round residents. So tiny is Virginia City that it is the only county seat in Montana that doesn't have a high school. But the population swells dramatically in the summer months when the town puts on its history face and embraces tourism.

With more than a dozen identifiable and restored historic sites concentrated within the town's boundaries, Virginia City rests at the intersection of three themes: focused, long-term historic restoration of structures and businesses, contemporary tourism outlets, and county seat functions. Modern activities, sprinkled along the historic pioneer town's restored main street, include a summer theater playhouse, walking tours, museums, gold panning, living history events, trail rides, and train rides.

Just about all the buildings on Wallace Street (State Highway 287) display false fronts typical of so many frontier towns. Cottonwood boardwalks line the street, in keeping with the architectural theme, and above the town to the west is its famous "boot hill." Among the many prominent historic sites are the Wells Fargo office, Montana Post building (1864), Masonic Hall (1867), Gilbert Brewery (1863), St. Mary's Hospital (now Bonanza Inn), Fairweather Inn (the remodeled Anaconda Hotel), Virginia City Opera House (in an old livery stable), Content's Corner (built in 1864, it served as the headquarters of the territorial government), as well as many vintage structures that have been carefully converted into brewpubs, artisan shops, bakeries, galleries, and restaurants.

Virginia City's life as a gold rush town was short lived. The town's population shrank as soon as newer diggings were found in Helena's Last Chance Gulch. Along with the exodus of miners went Virginia City's status as territorial capitol, which it ceded to Helena in 1875.

—PHOTO BY MICHAEL OBER

28

ELKHORN-COOLIDGE GHOST TOWN

45°29'41"N 113°02'29"W

Accessed from Forest Service Road 2465 off State Highway 43 in Beaverhead County

Montana's mining ghost towns can be found in the most improbable of places. Lacking easy access and far from transportation routes, they yielded their riches stubbornly. Coolidge, site of the Elkhorn Mine, is one example. The former silver-mining town conceals itself in the faraway reaches of the East Pioneer Mountains. Even today it is a 4-mile drive on a Forest Service road and a quarter-mile hike in. The townsite and its crumbling 138 structures, those that have not been scavenged or carted away, lie high in the valley of 10,046-foot Saddleback Mountain, where the processing building of the mine once clanked and groaned above miners' homes.

In the shrinking townsite there's the usual collection of collapsed wooden buildings. Against the hillside are the remains of a bunkhouse, one of nine, as well as a stable, chicken coop, ore bin, flume, and wood-framed privies. Along the creek is a building identified only as "pump house" by NRHP officials. Scattered 5-gallon tin canisters that held maple syrup tell the story of buying food goods in bulk because of the great distances to supply centers. Across the creek the concrete foundation piers of the mine's mill seem to glower upon the town that the mine spawned. The remains of the massive wooden superstructure that sat atop them, all five stories of it, were torn down in 2000. The mill housed a steam-heating plant, a sprinkler fire-protection system, and fifty-two electric motors that ran crushers, separators, dryers, and other equipment.

Like all mining communities, Coolidge had its share of barber shops, cigar stores, and hardware stores. There was even a pool hall. But no bars. The archaeological record and miners' accounts from the period indicate there were no taverns or brothels, an oddity for rough-and-tumble, male-dominated mining districts. The presence of tucked-away stills, however, indicate that the residents of Coolidge were supplied with ample spirits. The town is named for Calvin Coolidge, thought to have been an early investor in the mine.

To be profitable, the mine needed its own rail line to transport the ore. Completed in 1919 at a cost of 1.5 million dollars, the Montana Southern Railway followed the Big Hole River upstream from the town of Divide, and then headed up the Wise River to the mine. According to the official NRHP historical record, it was reportedly the last narrow-gauge railway built in the United States and was equipped with three Baldwin locomotives, twenty-eight freight cars, three passenger cars, a machine shop, an engine house, and depots.

In addition, the mine boasted its own unusual gravity-driven tramway from the mine tunnel at the upper camp to the mill. As cars loaded with ore descended the 1,450-foot-long tram, they pulled the empty cars back up.

—PHOTO BY US FOREST SERVICE

The Elkhorn Mine flourished between 1905 and 1920, in an era when men and women carried silver dollars in their pockets and purses. Compared to riskier silver mines scattered throughout western Montana, it was well funded by Eastern investors and European partners. It had sound management, modern equipment, a provable supply of ore, and stable infrastructure. When the silver market collapsed and investor backing disappeared, the mine and the town went dormant, never to recover. In 1927, a major flood on the Wise River severely disrupted rail and road access to the town and mine. Throughout the Depression both awaited the return of the silver market. Even up to 1946, inspections of the still intact mining equipment revealed that the mine could be operational with only small upgrades.

Starting in the mid-1970s a number of buildings were torn down for salvage lumber. But as late as 1975 the gigantic mill was still intact, along with the lower-camp sawmill, and in town, numerous buildings were still standing, though in serious disrepair. Today the majority of the Elkhorn-Coolidge Historic District's structures are badly deteriorated. Nonetheless, the NRHP nominating record states that it may be "the most intact and complete mine and mining camp site remaining in Montana. The fact that the mine, mill and town were kept in operating order up to the mid-1940s has meant that the processes of natural deterioration have had less effect than older abandoned mine sites." The historic district became an NRHP site in 2008, and small wooden markers and interpretive signs are scattered throughout it.

29

BUTTE-ANACONDA HISTORIC DISTRICT

46°00′55″N 112°32′10″W

Silver Bow County

Few towns in Montana wear their history more proudly than Butte. From a scattering of crude log cabins and tents in the early 1860s, to a boisterous and sprawling industrial metropolis, the storied citizens of Butte bent a mineral-rich hillside to their will. At its peak in 1917, the combined population of Butte, Anaconda, and surrounding Silver Bow County was estimated at 130,193, making it the largest metropolitan area between Minneapolis and Seattle. It was an epicenter for politics, ethnic diversity, labor relations, economics, and corporate power on both the state and national levels. With its staunch labor union–voting core, no presidential candidate ever skipped Butte while campaigning.

These days, though, the hollowed-out region can now claim only 25 percent of its former population. Its tycoons and power brokers long gone, its copper deposit exhausted, Butte now lives in a shrinking shadow of itself. Undaunted, Butte residents still embrace their heritage and, with uncompromising steadfastness, have kept a large section of uptown Butte preserved as a historic district. Sadly, much of what made Butte unique—its ethnic neighborhoods, working-class homes, bars, and brothels—has been gobbled up by the giant Berkeley Pit, the mine that made the town. Nevertheless, the Butte-Anaconda Historic District covers 9,774 total acres and contains 5,975 buildings of historic interest.

To document the district's resources for NRHP nomination, twenty-one historians worked many years cataloging the various qualifying resources in Butte and nearby Anaconda and Walkerville. The lengthy appendices identify hundreds of contributing structures that include residences from the Queen Anne, American craftsman, late Victorian, and Renaissance revival periods of architecture. Then there are the brick-and-stone commercial buildings in downtown Butte and Anaconda that represent their ascendency as metropolises. Finally, there are the stark headframes and assorted industrial mining remnants of the "richest hill on Earth."

Butte is often mischaracterized as a mining town that gathered all the evils of life and partook of little of the good. But as a place of nearly incomprehensible depth, the Butte-Anaconda Historic District requires a larger-than-life view of a mining town preserved by spirited citizens committed to saving a piece of their past. Butte, it is said, has always had a belief in tomorrow.

—PHOTOS BY STEVE WOODRUFF

30

ANACONDA SMOKESTACK

46°06′37″N 112°54′47″W

Southeast of Anaconda in Deer Lodge County

If industrial-scale smokestacks have a place in history, the Anaconda Smokestack tops them all. At 585 feet in height, the Washington Monument could fit inside of it. The stack is so big, it's said that a Volkswagen Beetle could drive around its wide lip. It looms over Anaconda, as if to forever remind the town of its deep connections with the Anaconda Copper Mining Company, or, simply, "the Company." Underneath the stack was the sprawling Washoe copper-smelting complex, built by the Anaconda Copper Mining Company in 1884. The stack itself was built in 1918, with the hope that its volume and height would solve Deer Lodge valley's pollution problems.

The smelter claimed the distinction of having the stack with the largest volume of any in the world. When in full operation, it discharged 3 to 4 million cubic feet of gas per minute. Unfortunately, as a result of the large capacity, the stack was ineffective at drafting. Company technicians installed a gas pipeline to heat the smoke to enable it to rise more rapidly, and down inside the smelter they deployed a complex array of devices to reduce the toxicity of the fumes that reached the stack. Despite these mitigations, the smelter dropped toxic amounts of sulfur dioxide and arsenic on the surrounding farmlands and forests, and the company endured endless rounds of lawsuits connected to this environmental pollution until the smelter was shuttered in 1980. The stack, largest in the world when completed, was the Anaconda Company's attempt to come up with a technical solution to likely the worst air pollution in the nation. Unfortunately, it resulted in only marginal success.

In the nominating documents for the NRHP, the authors summarize the importance of the stack "as a symbol of the complex industrial history of this one-company city for the people of Anaconda and as a monolithic reminder to the people of Montana of the unchallengeable power of the Company in the State's history." Now a lingering symbol of environmental pollution on a colossal scale, its legacy is the saint-to-sinner story. In the beginning it was lauded for bringing jobs to the region, but now it is remembered for environmental degradation. With the smelter now dismantled, the smokestack is the only structure to remain standing on the barren hill. The stack was donated to the Montana Department of Fish, Wildlife and Parks and is preserved both as a state park and an NRHP site.

—PHOTO BY STEVE WOODRUFF

31

METHODIST-EPISCOPAL CHURCH OF MARYSVILLE

46°45′05″N 112°17′58″W

On Third Street in Marysville in Lewis and Clark County

The Methodist-Episcopal Church of Marysville is the quintessential place of worship for a Montana mining town. Its functional clapboard siding, reflective of locally milled rough lumber, speaks to the utilitarian nature of mining communities of the late nineteenth century. It was a no-frills sanctuary in a lunch-bucket community.

The Drumlummon Mine in Marysville produced over 20 million dollars' worth of gold and silver, although its heyday was brief, spanning from 1886 to 1895. In 1886 while the mine was booming, an estimated five thousand people called Marysville home, with another five thousand scattered in adjacent mining sites. The town bustled with the comings and goings of thousands of souls bent on the singular task of digging gold and silver ore from the earth. Even though Marysville had two railroad lines, seven hotels, and numerous retail outlets, not to mention a brewery, twenty-six bars, and houses of ill-repute, its citizens still found a place for the church. Mining communities often constructed a church, both as an acknowledgment of their sinful leanings and to temper their rowdy reputation.

During its active years the church blended Methodist and Episcopal services. Because both denominations are Christian based and Bible centered, the blended order of worship and communion offered parishioners a common meeting ground. Since its construction in 1886, the one-room building has undergone numerous periods of repair and neglect. It is one of the most photographed churches in Montana.

—PHOTO BY MICHAEL OBER

32

J. C. ADAMS STONE BARN

47°32′25″N 111°41′11″W

Northeast of Sun River in Cascade County

In agricultural states like Montana there are plenty of barns, old and new, found in every corner of the state. The newer farm and ranch structures are more likely to be made of steel and have a low-profile roof, whereas older barns traditionally were made of wood and had a gambrel roof. And then there are the historic barns whose designs depart dramatically from tradition and modernity, such as the J. C. Adams Stone Barn in Sun River.

Arriving in Montana in 1864, the year it became a territory, J. C. Adams established himself as a competent freighter and livery man along the Mullan Road between Fort Benton and Helena. In 1872 he settled into a strategic homestead along the Sun River near the proposed site of the military post of Fort Shaw. In the ensuing years he expanded his stagecoach and freighting business to include vast cattle holdings to fulfill beef contracts with the growing garrison. To support these enterprises, he designed a magnificent stone barn. Because the ranch was situated in an area with scant timber, he hired Swedish stonecutters to harvest sandstone blocks from exposed bluffs near the Sun River and had them hauled on his freight wagons to his ranch headquarters. Between 1882 and 1885, the landmark barn, used as much for social functions as for storage for his wagons and shelter for his stock, took shape.

The barn featured three sections: the west portion was used for personal horses and tack; the center section sheltered cattle in the winter and during spring calving; the east end served as storage for wagons and buggies and as a meat locker for the beef that eventually headed to Fort Shaw. The entire second floor was used for social gatherings, parties, and celebrations, in addition to seasonal hay storage.

Adams lived until 1913, long enough to see his barn become a destination for curious travelers. Dogged by indebtedness, poor business decisions in other career ventures, and overextended mercantile and real estate investments, Adams withdrew from Montana to Chicago and left his ranch operations to his family members.

In the years that followed, J. C. Adams's widespread ranch holdings along the Sun River were split, sold, consolidated, and reorganized under a series of new owners. But the barn remained intact. In spite of a century of weathering, the sturdy barn still stands in a state of "arrested decay." Through the stewardship of neighbors, supportive owners, interested local citizens, and historical organizations the barn has experienced various levels of preservation and was granted its deserving place on the NRHP in 1979.

—PHOTO BY MICHAEL OBER

33

GILMAN STATE BANK

47°30′35″N 112°21′34″W

On Main Street in Gilman in Lewis and Clark County

Gilman State Bank is the last historic structure remaining in the former town of Gilman. It looks like what a rural Montana bank building in the early twentieth century should have looked like: sturdy, permanent, and secure. Its time as a bank, however, lasted only a decade. Today it's a renovated private residence—complete with preserved teller cage—amidst the leftovers of the former town, but its story is hitched to an unstable era of banking; the relationships between towns, banks, and railroads; and a feud with the town of Augusta, scarcely a five-minute drive west on US 287.

Chartering a bank in early twentieth-century Montana was easy, so aspiring entrepreneurs opened 397 new banks in the state, many of which were intended to serve the financial needs of the new communities like Gilman. A bank was a requisite element of stability for isolated rural towns. As railroads extended spur lines into remote areas, they created townsites along the way and offered a free lot to anyone who would charter and build a bank. Credit for depositors, often backed by the railroad, was readily available, as were loans. Depositors could establish accounts for as little as $5.

In 1912 Great Northern announced plans to build a branch line westward from Great Falls into the booming, irrigated benches of the Front Range along the Sun River. Instead of extending the line to the already established town of Augusta, the railroad built a station depot and town a short distance away and named it Gilman, after a former employee. And so the Gilman State Bank came to be, born of the premise that prosperity followed the railroad. Bit by bit, businesses and residents in Augusta migrated the 2 miles east to the new railroad town and its sturdy new bank, thinking Gilman was destined for big things.

But the town of Gilman lasted only ten years. By the early 1920s the bank had fallen on unsteady financial times. Unable to support ill-timed loans and bedeviled by the homestead collapse that plagued the state, Gilman State Bank closed in 1923, one of the 214 banks in Montana that failed during the early years of the 1920s.

Then, in an ironic reversal of fortunes, the Great Northern extended its tracks to Augusta, leaving Gilman—and its shuttered bank—behind. Almost overnight, Gilman died. Many businesses and homes were carted back to Augusta, some on sledges in the winter and some disassembled and placed on wagons or farm trucks. Eventually, even the railroad pulled out. Today, neither Augusta nor Gilman has a railroad. Or a bank.

—PHOTO BY STEVE WOODRUFF

34

IZAAK WALTON INN

48°16′43″N 113°36′41″W

On US 2 in Essex in Flathead County

It is hard to deny the strong railroading element of the Izaak Walton Inn. Perched just a short distance from the Burlington Northern's transcontinental train tracks, it beams with transportation history. An unmistakable railroadiana theme permeates the entire structure and grounds. The walls are adorned with vintage photos of trains, train wrecks, track crews, snowsheds, and blizzards. The lobby, dining room, and downstairs bar feature relics like semaphores, signal lights, signs, and tools.

Built in 1939, the Great Northern Railway's motives with the inn were largely corporate driven, with a side nod to summer guests. It was meant to be more a boardinghouse than a tourist destination. The original twenty-nine bedrooms and ten bathrooms were designed to be occupied by hotel staff and railroad employees: track crews, steam pipe fitters, coalers, "B and B" (bridges and buildings) carpenters, trainmasters, mechanics, and gandy dancers. Large crews of up to sixty men each were especially needed in the winter months. In the summer they were deployed elsewhere when the inn catered to summer tourists visiting Glacier National Park. It took a crew of only twelve carpenters three months to complete the Tudor revival–style structure that included a lobby and fireplace, a lunchroom, and a kitchen with a 2-ton stove.

With the advent of modernized snow-removal equipment and more efficient trackage and rolling stock, the need for large railroad crews diminished, so the hotel transitioned to a full-time, year-round tourist facility. In 1950, the railroad sold the building to private owners who focused exclusively on the tourist trade.

Since the beginning, it has been the only year-round tourist facility serving travelers along US 2 adjacent to the park. Today, the inn takes its trade from a steady supply of summer and winter clientele. Around the hotel and parallel to the tracks, the small community of Essex arose, first as a railroad-servicing center, and more recently as a charming summer resort and winter recreation mecca for skiers and snowmobilers. Deep snow is the rule here—fun for winter recreationalists today but daunting for the track-maintenance crews of the past, who were grateful for the serviceable inn's warmth and shelter.

The Izaak Walton Inn is named for the celebrated fly fisherman and English author Izaak Walton in a loose but likely association to the nearby Middle Fork of the Flathead River. The Flathead River system and Glacier National Park have deep connections with trout anglers. The hotel was listed as an NRHP site in 1985.

—PHOTO BY MICHAEL OBER

35

WURTZ HOMESTEAD

48°53′55″N 114°23′19″W

Along the North Fork Road in Flathead County

Even today, the term "up the North Fork" tells of a place—the North Fork of the Flathead River valley—that is otherworldly. Remote, isolated, and almost always covered with deep snow well into spring, residents of one hundred years ago lived a life in stark contrast to that of the sodbusters of the open plains of eastern Montana.

In spite of the region's remoteness and winter weather, more than one thousand homestead claims were filed for land west of the North Fork River between 1910 and the start of World War I, attesting to the determination of pioneers taking advantage of the Enlarged Homestead Act of 1909. Frank and Ella Wurtz, Midwest transplants, were among those seeking a better life. Frank claimed 160 acres in 1913, began to clear land for cultivation, and started to construct a log home for his growing family. The Wurtzes and other hopeful homesteaders up and down the North Fork of the Flathead River valley spent toilsome days hacking farmland and grazing fields out of forests. Many of the open glens and meadows of the North Fork today were made during the homestead era. In truth, most homesteaders here never achieved anything other than bare subsistence farming.

An ongoing dispute between Wurtz and US Forest Service officials over the validity of his land claim plagued him and his family during their initial years, but they persevered. They spent winters in Kalispell, where Frank worked in lumber and flour mills, returning to the North Fork each summer to build additional log buildings on their homestead, to cultivate a horse pasture, and to clear trees. Adding to this already burdensome lifestyle, the original log cabin burned in 1919, and two of their three children weren't found afterward—not even their bodies. Arson and kidnapping were suspected. In 1920, Frank succeeded in certifying his claim to the land and set about building his final log house, but Ella, gripped by the loss of two children, insisted that they move to Washington state.

It was 1932 before they returned to their North Fork property, only to find that the two remaining buildings, thought abandoned, had been taken over by the school district for use as a school, and all their possessions had disappeared, setting off another dispute over ownership. Eventually Frank proved ownership through property tax records, and he completed the cabin that he had started thirteen years earlier. With minor modifications over the years, it stands today. The Wurtzes sold the homestead property in 1964, and the Flathead National Forest acquired the land in 1990 and stabilized and restored two of the main original buildings. The homestead was entered into the NRHP in 1996.

Today the Wurtz buildings serve as rental cabins of the Flathead National Forest. The bucolic charm of the site belies its troubled history—the hardships and challenges the Wurtzes experienced. It tells an incomplete story of a time when good luck favored only a few.

—PHOTO BY MICHAEL OBER

36

KEVIN DEPOT

48°44′45″N 111°58′04″W

At Central Avenue and First Street in Kevin in Toole County

At the peak of Montana's great railroad era, between the 1920s and 1930s, dozens of small train stations dotted the landscape, sitting adjacent to the main lines, branch lines, and short-haul lines—transportation corridors that are mostly gone now. Their train platforms, ticket windows, and waiting rooms were the gateway into—and out of—tiny towns. Clinging to the rails like barnacles to a hull, these small rural train stations each had an accoutrement of similarly arranged buildings: water tower, grain elevator, section-hands bunkhouse, and pumphouse. In isolated whistle-stop towns, the railroad depot served as the community town hall, and it was the railroad telegrapher who sent and received news before electricity or radios. The Kevin Depot, in north-central Montana, is one of the survivors of this era. It was placed on the NRHP in 1979.

Like most rural depots, the Kevin Depot eschews grand architecture over function. Its single-floor layout served as a ticket counter, freight-sorting area, telegraph office, and waiting room with a central stove and brick chimney for heat. There were spartan quarters for the station agent, who also worked as a freight and baggage handler, ticket agent, and relief telegrapher. The Great Northern Railway, the rail line that snaked its way across northern Montana, a region referred to as the Hi-Line, built the depot to service its steam locomotives with water on their way to Canada. Rainwater, collected in a pit behind the station, was pumped into a water tower. The "bump out" telegrapher's station featured windows that faced the tracks and afforded a view of arriving and departing trains. This standard architectural footprint was repeated all across Montana.

In 1922, an oil boom hit northern Montana, and, because of the rail stop at Kevin, the town also boomed. In the 1930s, however, the Great Northern discontinued passenger trains on its run to Canada, thereby eliminating the need for a ticket agent and station manager at Kevin. The town collapsed and emptied out. In other small towns along the Hi-Line, such as Sunburst, Galata, and Sweetgrass, the Great Northern began decommissioning and razing similar depots in the 1960s.

In 1975, the railroad abandoned the Kevin Depot altogether. The new owners, Burlington Northern, announced plans to demolish it, but the Kevin Economic Development Corporation put on a resolute face and determined that the depot would not be relegated to the dustbin of history. It successfully acquired the building and moved the depot two blocks away, still within sight of the rail right-of-way. Unburdened by time and embracing its new future, it survives as a senior citizens center.

—PHOTO BY STEVE WOODRUFF

37

VIRGELLE MERCANTILE AND BANK

48°00′57″N 110°14′55″W

On County Road 430, about 6 miles south of US 87 in Chouteau County

Virgil Blankenbaker moved from Missouri to Montana's endless expanses in 1886, just in time to witness the collapse of the mighty open-range cattle industry that disastrous winter. Thinking sheep might be a better grazing animal, he went into business with some of his relatives in north-central Montana. Together, they expanded their herds, acquired more land, and prospered.

The Blankenbaker family's story is an uncommon one from the homestead era, when most "honyockers" failed as dryland farmers. They, however, located their ranch holdings on the soil-rich Missouri River bottomlands and, from there, built an empire that extended 15 miles upstream and downstream. By good fortune, the Great Northern Railway routed a branch line between Havre and Great Falls that passed near their home, further securing their commercial base. Then came the post office, with Virgil appointed postmaster. With the river, the railroad, the post office, and an increasing number of neighbors, Virgil thought it prudent to establish a mercantile business in 1912. The next year, he contracted to have a ferry built on the Missouri River, less than a mile from his mercantile. He also built and managed a local lumberyard. Along with productive crops during the wet years of the early homestead era came the need to establish a local bank. So, Virgil chartered one—next to his mercantile and made of sturdy bricks.

For many years, the small community of Virgelle, named for Virgil and his wife, Ella, who was also his cousin, was the focal point for local events, such as baseball games, picnics, political rallies, and speeches. Things were fruitful until the drought came in 1917, and grain prices fell after World War I. The subsequent dry years drove farmers away, and the mercantile struggled to stay open after neighbors began driving their Model Ts to nearby Fort Benton or Great Falls to buy goods. The bank closed in 1927 and became a community center and dance hall. Ever the entrepreneur, Virgil Blankenbaker bought up nearby bankrupt farmsteads and expanded his ranch into one of the two largest in Chouteau County. He served two terms in the state legislature and died in an auto accident in 1936. Ella died in 1940.

Only two structures from the former Blankenbaker empire—the bank and the mercantile—remain in Virgelle. The Virgelle Mercantile is now an antique store and bed-and-breakfast, complete with restored rooms furnished with period-appropriate antiques. Outside the mercantile are reclaimed homesteader shacks brought in to augment its rented rooms. The original icehouse has been converted into a shower house. Lush crop fields still spread across the broad bottomlands of the Missouri River below the Virgelle Mercantile today, a scene that Virgil Blankenbaker would take pleasure in.

—PHOTO COURTESY VIRGELLE MERCANTILE

38

DAVE'S TEXACO

48°35′35″N 109°13′54″W

At 237 Pennsylvania Street in Chinook in Blaine County

"Fill 'er up" and "Check the oil" were once part of our vehicular vernacular, phrases stemming from the early and mid-twentieth century, when traveling Americans drove on small two-lane highways, decades ahead of interstates. The town service station served as the primary service source for these Americans' vehicles, for either fueling or fixing. And for small rural areas like Chinook, the local service station was often the social gathering place for town and country folk.

In a scene more befitting a 1930s Hollywood movie set, Dave's Texaco remains rooted in place, where its original aim was to draw business from travelers on the new Theodore Roosevelt International Highway (US 2), the Montana portion of which stretched along the Hi-Line. Built in 1927, Dave's Texaco is one of only a few 1920s-era service stations that maintain their original façade and footprint. Between 1929 and 1939, the number of filling stations across Montana grew from 438 to 1,349. Dave's Texaco was at the head of that trend. The expanding automobile and gasoline-powered farm machinery industries reflected a nation that was becoming mechanized and mobile—and the filling stations followed the boom.

According to the NRHP nominating document, "Architecturally, the building is one of the finest examples of the domestic or cottage style design in the northwestern United States. When viewed from the exterior or interior, the unaltered integrity of the building is amazing." Though the station no longer pumps gas, recent alterations have been kept to a minimum. One of the station's original gasoline pumps still boasts its Texaco globes. Dave's Texaco, as it was known for over forty years, provided motorists with homegrown service for more than sixty-five years. It joined the NRHP in 1994.

—PHOTOS BY STEVE WOODRUFF

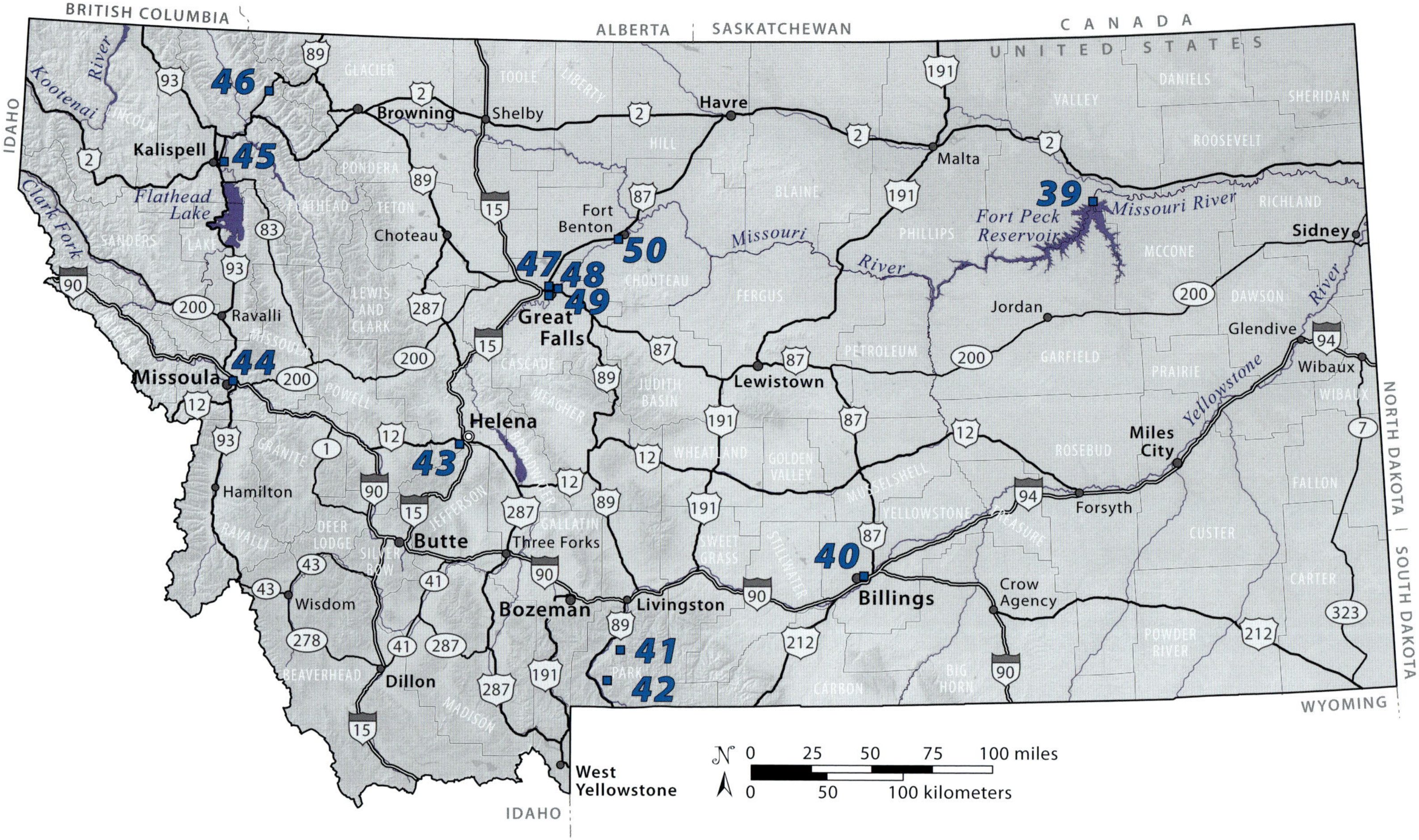

39 Fort Peck Theatre
40 Moss Mansion
41 Chico Hot Springs
42 OTO Homestead and Dude Ranch
43 Cathedral of St. Helena
44 University Apartments
45 Conrad Mansion
46 *DeSmet* Tour Boat
47 Chicago, Milwaukee, and St. Paul Depot
48 Charles M. Russell Home
49 Tenth Street Bridge
50 Grand Union Hotel

Grand Visions

As Montana became settled, it put its social face on, enshrined in the tangible emergence of hotels, theaters, and mansions. It gathered such physical trappings as if to exclaim its right to statehood. The built landscape of successive years represented the citizenry's best foot forward. Some of those visionary efforts resulted in now-preserved structures of the early nineteenth century and celebrated places that took the dare and succeeded. These selected sites reflect a maturing and prideful population. Those who built them were ever aware that the design and value of those structures were a signal to others, including tourists and prominent visitors, of wealth, stability, and permanence. Their social nature—and larger-than-life footprints—tell of a time when Montana had come of age.

The Hotel Meade in the Bannack Historic Dristrict. —PHOTO BY STEVE WOODRUFF

39

FORT PECK THEATRE

48°00′27″N 106°27′00″W

On Missouri Avenue in Fort Peck in Valley County

Cheers and jeers arose from the balcony and lower seating of the Fort Peck Theatre as moviegoers viewed *Mutiny on the Bounty*, starring Charles Laughton and Clark Gable, in 1935. At the movie's conclusion, they all went home to their shanty shacks or tents, and in the morning they resumed work on the world's largest earth-filled dam—at fifty cents an hour. Such was life in Fort Peck at the peak of the Great Depression, as men toiled away at one of the New Deal's largest Works Progress Administration (WPA) projects ever undertaken.

Construction towns like Wheeler, New Deal, and Delano Heights sprang up all around the dam site. These were fast times in the little hard-shelled communities, where men found steady wages at a time when most folks couldn't scratch up a nickel. The largest town, though, was Fort Peck itself. With nearly ten thousand residents, it boasted a hospital, recreation center, school, curved streets and sidewalks, cafés and grocery stores, and playgrounds. The construction town also had its share of bars and bowling alleys—and brothels—for the mostly male population. But the real epicenter of entertainment for the round-the-clock workers was the theatre, a massive 1,209-seat performing stage and movie venue.

Just as the New Deal's WPA programs were aimed at healing the nation's Depression ills, the theatre was designed to break up the monotony and tedium of the weary workers' days. But the theatre wasn't just for screening films; it also hosted town hall meetings, church services, play productions, and concerts.

Now fully restored, the theatre is a destination site for live-theatre enthusiasts in the summer. In period-perfect décor, its Swiss chalet–style architecture is best described in the narrative accompanying the NRHP nomination form:

> The careful attention to detail, from the cut-out balustrades, false balconies, chamfered beams, hand-crafted lighting fixtures, herringbone siding pattern, decorative vergeboard, and interior rustic finish, lends the Theatre a whimsical quality that is most unusual in WPA construction and unsurpassed in Montana.

As a bonus to visiting history buffs, the nearby dam has a visitor center, and both the Fort Peck Original Houses Historic District and Fort Peck Dam itself are listed on the NRHP. Both are worthy locations for seeing Depression-era architecture.

—PHOTO COURTESY FORK PECK FINE ARTS COUNCIL, INC.

40

MOSS MANSION

44°46′46″N 108°30′55″W

At 914 Division Street in Billings in Yellowstone County

Preston B. Moss made a sizable fortune selling one of Montana's most abundant natural resources: water. He was instrumental in building the BL&I Canal in 1905 that irrigated the 40,000-acre Billings Bench. With its series of flumes, canals, and ditches with intricate headgates and flow-measuring valves, the canal brought water to the growing city of Billings. His "Big Ditch" was a replica of the one designed by Brigham Young in Utah.

But Moss's economic interests were diversified beyond his irrigation projects. In partnership with neighbors and other investors, he owned eighty thousand head of sheep and several thousand head of cattle, built the Northern Hotel, and was an incorporator of the one-million-dollar Billings Sugar Factory. "PB," as he was known, founded the *Billings Evening Journal* and merged it with the *Billings Gazette*, operated the city's central steam plant, organized the first automatic dial phone system in Montana, built Billings' first meat-packing plant, and helped start Rocky Mountain College. He even started a toothpaste factory that employed bentonite in its formula.

To crown his achievements, Moss built an 11,000-square-foot, 23-room, 3-story mansion at the edge of town, on farmland irrigated by his canal. Built of Lake Superior red sandstone, the home was completed in 1903 for his wife, Martha, and their five children and three servants. The home is a blend of numerous decorative styles, from its art rococo French parlor to the Moorish entry. There is an art nouveau sitting room, and the dining room is a mini oak sanctuary styled after the Plaza Hotel in New York City. The building had hot and cold indoor running water on all three floors, an early rotary telephone that connected Moss to his downtown business office, and an electric bell system for the servants.

Today, the Moss Mansion survives as a museum, completely intact and reflective of the life and times of Billings' most diversified business and civic leader. The city of Billings and the state of Montana own it jointly, and it is managed by the Billings Preservation Society. It was listed on the NRHP in 1982. It is open to the public, at the wishes of the family. The mansion is preserved with original Persian carpets and window drapes, wall art, furnishings, and meticulously manicured grounds. All around it are the quiet residential neighborhoods of Billings, which developed alongside PB's fortunes.

—PHOTO COURTESY CLARK MARTEN

41

CHICO HOT SPRINGS

45°20′10″N 110°41′35″W

Off US 89 southeast of Emigrant in Park County

Long before there was a Yellowstone National Park, with its notable geysers and hot pools, and long before there were passable tote roads or a rail line, gold miners crawled up and down Emigrant Gulch in search of fresh finds. In their wanderings for gold they found another form of wealth: natural hot springs. Chico Hot Springs got its start during this territorial mining period, primarily as a place for bone-weary placer miners to soak and bathe.

In his January 16, 1865, diary entry, John S. Hackney offered the first recorded visit to the hot springs: "Went out to the hot springs and washed my dirty 'duds.'" According to the NRHP nominating documents, the hot springs were named for an animated Mexican man who regaled miners in Emigrant, in 1866, with stories of the wonders of Yellowstone, which he and five others had just traveled through. Apparently, he was remembered two years later when the mail drop in Emigrant was named after him. Also in 1866, local gold miners built a concrete box at the hot springs site to capture some of the consistent 112-degree geothermal water. An official post office was established in 1874, and in 1877 the Chico School was built. In the late 1890s, a boardinghouse was built; it accommodated a dozen of the local miners with six-dollar-a-week rooms and hearty meals. In 1900, a hotel building was built at the springs, and Chico was on its way to becoming the premier resort hot springs in the new state of Montana. In constructing the main lodge, the owners sought to move from the wall-tent-and-boardinghouse era to a classic resort centered around a charming white Georgian revival hotel with dormers and a veranda. On June 20, 1900, the forty-guest hotel officially opened, with "big jollification," according to the *Livingston Enterprise*. The hot springs had a central "hot plunge," as well as 6-foot-deep soaking pools next to a 9-foot-deep swimming pool.

Interest in the West, aided by the completion of transcontinental railways, drew tourists to southwest Montana. Chico catered to travelers from the East seeking the relaxation of a good resort and the benefits of a hot springs health "plunge." Charlie Russell was a regular guest. So were many dignitaries from Europe. Governors and legislators scheduled business meetings there. Teddy Roosevelt stopped over on his way to dedicate the Roosevelt Arch at the entrance to Yellowstone National Park.

For a time, Chico also served as the local hospital. Owing to the restorative nature of the natural mineral springs, owners billed the resort as a place for relief from ailments such as rheumatism, arthritis, and stomach and kidney disorders. In 1916, a fully functioning doctor's office and hospital were integrated into the hot springs' business model, and by 1920, the

—PHOTO BY LYNN DONALDSON

hospital had admitted 2,390 patients, performed 935 surgeries, and birthed 32 babies. Chico served in this capacity until newer health care facilities were constructed in Livingston.

Over the decades Chico has seen a string of owners buffeted by the whims of the traveling public, the Depression years, Prohibition, undercapitalization, and poor management. Through these years, though, the business continued to grow while other resorts closed. The original spring site remains today, and the faithful flow continues to be directed to the pools and heating system of one of Montana's most celebrated and continually operating hot springs resorts. The original lilac bushes and landscaped trees surrounding the original main lodge have matured into graceful grounds, and the carefully restored building is appointed with period furnishings that make it the centerpiece of this historic site. Chico Hot Springs became an NRHP site in 1998.

42

OTO HOMESTEAD AND DUDE RANCH

45°08′56″N 110°46′55″W

Along Cedar Creek 15 miles north of Gardiner in Park County

Chain motels, bed-and-breakfasts, and vacation rentals are common fare for today's visitors to Montana. But there was a time, particularly in the 1920s and 30s, when a vacation at a Western dude ranch was the crème de la crème for wealthy visitors. The OTO Dude Ranch was constructed to meet the needs of just these guests: well-heeled rail-borne tourists from the East seeking to experience a rustic ranch-style vacation.

The OTO began as a small and unpromising cattle ranch. Dick and Dora Randall acquired the parcel of bottomland alongside Cedar Creek in 1898, which included a one-room log cabin reportedly used by stage robbers. They scratched in a small vegetable garden out back behind the dirt-floored, sod-roofed cabin. For ten years prior to their purchase, Dick had worked as a stagecoach driver in Yellowstone, ferrying guests to and from the park's massive log hotels. Believing he could capitalize on the tourist industry in the Gardiner area, he and his wife converted the homestead and cattle operations into a guest facility offering a true "old West" theme recalling cattle ranch days of the open range. The OTO became the first dude ranch in Montana. "Combining dudes with cows," according to Roberta Cheney in *Music, Saddles, and Flapjacks*, "was the best way to make a cattle ranch pay." The fact that the OTO was near Gardiner, on a spur line of the transcontinental Northern Pacific Railway, aided their success. The Gardiner passenger depot was the jumping-off place for visitors to Yellowstone National Park and nearby guest ranches in the Gallatin National Forest.

Between 1912 and 1934 they expanded their operations to include a massive log lodge with guest rooms, a dining area, and numerous small log guest cabins. For a while, the ranch even had its own post office. From this central base, guests could ride horses into the Gallatin National Forest, fish, hunt, hike, enjoy hayrides, partake in open-air and open-fire dinners, target shoot, picnic, and listen to old-fashioned Western campfire music. Their guests included many dignitaries, politicians, foreign officials, statesmen, moguls of industry, and movie stars. Many families spent the entire summer at the ranch. Come fall, Dick guided hunting trips deep into the national forest. The Randalls were the pioneers of Montana's leisure and hospitality industry.

Business fell off during the Great Depression, and the Randalls retired and sold the ranch to a former guest who suffered the same business insolvency. It closed in 1939, never to reopen as a dude ranch. For three decades after it closed, it was a private horse and cattle ranch. The former dude ranch structures and equipment, in varying stages of abandonment and decay, and much of the adjoining acreage are now part of the Gallatin National Forest, open to the public. In 2004 the site was listed on the NRHP, and volunteer groups continue to renovate the principal structures to prevent further decline.

—PHOTO BY MICHAEL OBER

43

CATHEDRAL OF SAINT HELENA

46°35′25″N 112°01′57″W

At 530 North Ewing Street in Helena in Lewis and Clark County

From just about any approach to Helena, the twin spires of the Cathedral of Saint Helena can be seen rising heavenward 230 feet. The cathedral is the tallest building in Helena. It is one of the city's most celebrated physical landmarks, along with the state capitol.

In architectural grandeur alone, the cathedral earns its place on the NRHP. It was designed to resemble the impressive cathedral of Cologne, Germany, and is a close replica of the Votive Church of Vienna. Like many Gothic churches throughout Europe, its plan forms a cross. Two stories of stained glass windows grace the exterior, totaling 11,696 square feet of art glass. Fifty-nine of the windows, crafted in Bavaria, portray events from the Old and New Testaments and later church history. The matching towering spires are clad with Indiana limestone and topped with red-tiled, steeply pitched roofs. From the north tower, the chimes of fifteen hand-cast bells forged in a Baltimore foundry ring down upon the historic Last Chance Gulch below, calling worshippers to service. The cathedral occupies an entire block on a hill above the downtown business district and surrounding residential neighborhoods.

By the time of its first Mass in 1914, many of Helena's wealthy and elite had contributed to its lengthy construction period. Foremost among them was Thomas Cruse, a tough-minded Irish-Catholic prospector who discovered the Drumlummon lode, established the town of Marysville, and became one of the most prominent figures in Montana's mining history. He passed away a month after the first Mass. Fittingly, his was the first funeral held at the cathedral. Other financial contributors included Senator Thomas J. Walsh, Thomas C. Power, and Bishop John P. Carroll, who established Carroll College in Helena. As noted in the narrative accompanying the NRHP nomination form, the town of Helena had a suitable number of ingredients to construct a church of such a grand scale: highly skilled laborers from nearby mines, a great concentration of wealthy citizens, plentiful building materials, and an endless sense of community pride and confidence.

Following its first Mass, intensive construction continued until the cathedral's final dedication in 1924. In the years since, the Catholic Diocese of Helena has authorized several renovation efforts, most notably those aimed at repairing significant damage following a 1935 earthquake. The Cathedral of Saint Helena was added to the NRHP in 1980.

—PHOTO BY MICHAEL OBER

44

UNIVERSITY APARTMENTS

46°51′45″N 113°59′48″W

The 400 block of Roosevelt Street in Missoula in Missoula County

The University Apartments building in Missoula, designed by A. J. Gibson, recalls the early 1900s Boston brownstones. If the walls of the two-story, twelve-unit apartment complex could talk, they would tell stories of the city of Missoula developing over the last century.

In the early 1900s, Missoula's core business and residential districts were north of the Clark Fork River. On the flats to the southeast at the base of Mount Sentinel stood the beginnings of the University of Montana, then just a remote cluster of buildings. The apartments were built in the transitional zone between the two districts at a time when Missoula was experiencing active development. Newspaper accounts tell of "gala balls" and "festive dinners" at the apartments, hosted by the emerging professional class of Missoulians and attended by prominent town officials. Missoula was prospering at the time with its lucrative lumber industry, agriculture, and fledgling university.

Around the apartments Missoula spread out, claiming the open flats on both sides of the river. Over the years many owners, merchants, and commercial workers emerged from the apartments and fulfilled their roles in the town's business sector. Likewise, generations of university students, from post–World War II veterans to bobby-socked young ladies in the fifties to bell-bottomed kids in the seventies and on to contemporary times, marched off to campus classes, passing through the columnar entrance porticos.

As much as anything, these apartments, with their neoclassic details, reflect the talent of Albert J. Gibson, Missoula's best-known architect at the turn of the century. The structures he designed in the late 1800s and early 1900s symbolized Missoula's rapid development. He drew plans for the Greenough residence, a large Queen Anne–style home; the Gustav Peterson home and Gibson Mansion, neoclassic style residences; and public and institutional buildings reflected in the design of the Carnegie Library.

The University Apartments were constructed in 1909 for Charles E. Johnson, a cement contractor who owned the property from 1908 to 1910. They were the last of Gibson's architectural efforts; he retired after designing them and focused on his passion for automobiles—racing and touring. He and his wife died in December 1927 when a train struck their car near Missoula. Today these apartments are still considered a special place for history-minded Missoulians. They joined the NRHP in 1985.

—PHOTO BY STEVE WOODRUFF

45

CONRAD MANSION

48°11′49″N 114°18′08″W

At 313 Sixth Avenue East in Kalispell in Flathead County

It has been said that the brothers William and Charles Conrad stepped off the gangplank of a steamboat in Fort Benton, each having only half interest in a silver dollar. Though likely apocryphal, if true their story is a remarkable saga of luck, pluck, determination, and good business savvy that turned poverty into fabulous wealth.

The two brothers left their war-ravaged family plantation in the Shenandoah Valley in 1868, when the youngest, Charles E. Conrad, was only eighteen. Setting their sights on the unsettled territory of Montana, they booked passage on a steamboat and began a five-week journey up the Missouri River. Using Fort Benton as a base, the brothers engaged in the emerging businesses of freighting and riverboat shipping. Eventually they split up, both destined for parallel lives of fortune. Charles settled in the Flathead Valley and laid out the plats for the emerging town of Kalispell. He extended his business empire to include banking, real estate, ranching, and mining in both Montana and Canada.

To complement his successful empire, he hired the Spokane architectural firm of Kirtland Cutter, designers of the Davenport Hotel in Spokane and Lake McDonald Lodge in Glacier National Park, to generate the plans for a twenty-three-room, eight-fireplace, Norman-style mansion with an elevator linking all three floors. Completed in 1895, it became the hub of formal gatherings for the growing town.

The Conrads entertained frequently and lavishly. The great home was the scene of many parties, and the social life of Kalispell revolved around the gregarious Conrad family. Dignitaries and leaders in many fields were often guests at the mansion, including the artist Charles M. Russell, conservationist and zoologist W. T. Hornaday, physician and explorer Lyman B. Sperry, naturalist George Bird Grinnell, railroader James J. Hill, and President Theodore Roosevelt.

In a time when the wealthy built homes befitting their stature, the Conrad Mansion served as the anchor point for Kalispell's growth and denoted Conrad's influence over the town's culture and economy. Fittingly, it is now the property of the city of Kalispell and, as a true-to-period living museum in restored condition, is a destination for tourists and townspeople. The grounds have been tastefully landscaped to reflect their former opulence but do not completely mirror the expansive estate the Conrad family once controlled, which included a carriage house, stables, a buffalo paddock, a game preserve, and orchards. Remnants of an encircling native stone fence, built by European stonemasons without mortar, frame the manicured yard.

—PHOTO COURTESY CONRAD MANSION

Inside, the central Great Room is joined by a fernery with an indoor stream and pond, a music room, a library, a billiard room, a formal dining room, a grandmother's quarters, and playrooms for kids. Two water fountains supplied ice-chilled water for guests in the summer. The laundry, normally located in the basement of such homes, had to be plumbed to the third floor due to problems with drainage and a high water table. The pine "plat table," originally belonging to the Kalispell Townsite Company and which was used to lay out the town of Kalispell, also resides in the mansion, as Charles spearheaded the campaign to make the town the centerpiece of commercial development in the valley. The majority of the mansion's furnishings are period originals, acquired during the financial panic of 1883 at bargain prices back East and shipped to Montana. The Conrads are the only family to have lived in the home. Open to the public, the Conrad Mansion encapsulates the Conrad family's rags-to-riches story. It has been an NRHP site since 1975.

46

DeSmet Tour Boat

48°37′04″N 113°52′47″W

On Lake McDonald in Glacier National Park in Flathead County

A countless number of young men and women have held coveted summer jobs as captains and deckhands on the tour boat *DeSmet* in Glacier National Park. The wooden, 56-foot-long, 70-passenger US Coast Guard–registered vessel has spent its entire life on the park's Lake McDonald, providing scenic tours for thousands of Glacier's visitors, and not a few weddings, receptions, reunions, and other lake-centered social events.

Though not a fixed-in-place object like most other listees on the NRHP, this floating site has a unique historic legacy of its own. Built in 1930 by J. W. "Billy" Swanson, it is named for Pierre-Jean De Smet, a noted Montana Jesuit missionary from the mid-nineteenth century. Since 1930 it has provided ninety years of continuous safe and nostalgic travel over the waters of Lake McDonald.

The *DeSmet*'s carvel-planked hull design reflects tour boat architecture of the period, making it a floating maritime museum of exquisite integrity. It features an oak-ribbed, cedar-planked hull trimmed with fir and oak, as well as an oak maritime steering wheel. Owners through time have faithfully retained the look and feel of the now-gone wooden-boat era.

In describing the technical nature of maintaining this unique site, writers of the NRHP nomination papers wrote:

> Over the years, repairs have mostly followed traditional methods and the overall design has not been changed. The boat still maintains a large amount of original materials in both the hull and superstructure. New steam bent oak frames have either replaced or been "sistered" to those too deteriorated to serve inside the hull. New fir has been used to replace rotten areas of the original fir stem and keel. Areas of the hull require new cedar planks on a regular basis due to the persistence of rot associated with annual swelling and drying of the wood planks. All new planks are of locally-sourced cedar and follow the same lines as the original layout.

In 1979, its original gasoline engine was replaced by a four-cylinder Perkins diesel engine. The boat is dry-docked and stored in its own boathouse (also listed on the NRHP) at the foot of Lake McDonald. Each spring, it emerges for fresh paint and needed overhauls by craftsmen and boatwrights before being inspected and placed into service.

As the nomination papers make clear, the historic attributes of the *DeSmet* make its placement in the NRHP a natural choice. The boat "serves as a time transport machine taking passengers back to when the fledgling boat concession provided a unique and different view of the park, a view from the water to the land." The *DeSmet* is joined on the NRHP by three sister boats that ply Glacier National Park's waters: the *Little Chief*, *Morning Eagle*, and *Sinopah*.

—PHOTO BY HUNTER D'ANTUONO, *FLATHEAD BEACON*

47

CHICAGO, MILWAUKEE, AND ST. PAUL PASSENGER DEPOT

47°30'25"N 111°18'29"W

On River Drive in Great Falls in Cascade County

By the mid-1920s rail lines had reached nearly all of Montana's well-settled parts through an extensive array of main and branch routes. All three of the national transcontinental railroads—the Milwaukee Road, Great Northern, and Northern Pacific—constructed giant, monolithic train stations in each of Montana's six largest cities. These imposing buildings symbolize the great railroad era of the early twentieth century.

Built of bricks to represent the power of the industrial giants of that transportation period, these depots differed markedly from the dozens of smaller, less-imposing wooden depots (see Kevin Depot) found across the state. Urban stations were different because of the wider array of traveler services they provided, including commodious waiting rooms, newsstands, sophisticated heating systems, smoking rooms, lunch counters (often referred to as "the beanery"), and faster connections to other stations. Their impressive size and complicated rooflines and towers dominated their respective cityscapes, so they served as much for advertising as for function. Most of these larger stations featured a clock tower, often with four clock faces looking in four different directions to remind townsfolks and travelers of the faithful timeliness of their railroad schedules.

The Chicago, Milwaukee, and St. Paul Passenger Depot in Great Falls features a 135-foot-tall tower, still bearing the Milwaukee Road's insignia. It looms over the downtown and slow-moving Missouri River. The station was constructed in 1915. According to the NRHP nomination form, "The architectural significance of the building is substantiated by its exquisite proportions, the incorporation of Mission style detailing, and the high degree of originality and sophistication evident in the design. It is one of the finest examples of early 20th Century railroad station architecture in Montana and compares favorably with the Milwaukee Road's depots in Missoula and Butte." Contributing historic elements include stained glass windows, marble floors, and extensive original woodwork. Outside, the brick facings, groomed grounds, and tall windows attest to Great Fall's railroad beginnings.

During the 1960s the Milwaukee Road began phasing out its freight and passenger operations at the Great Falls station. The troubled rail line went bankrupt for the last time in 1980. Vacant for many years, the train station underwent

—PHOTO BY STEVE WOODRUFF

renovations to become an indoor shopping mall in the 1970s. It qualified for and was placed on the NRHP in 1988.

Today, the railroad tracks have long since been removed, and the grounds facing the river have been landscaped as a public park. A riverfront bike trail and footpath follow much of the former track right-of-way. Inside, the massive two-story station has been converted into executive office suites. Outside, the proud square tower still dominates the windy skyscape of Great Falls.

48

CHARLES M. RUSSELL HOUSE AND STUDIO

47°30′36″N 111°17′05″W

At 1217–1219 Fourth Avenue North in Great Falls in Cascade County

Nothing evokes "Montana" in larger letters than Charles Marion Russell. Montanans and scores of Western art lovers around the world celebrate his life and well-known works. A statue of him is displayed in Statuary Hall in the State Capitol, alongside Jeanette Rankin, both individuals who best represent the state and its values.

His artistic talent was unique in that he did not focus on just one medium. Russell was equally at ease with pencil sketches, clay models, large-scale oils and watercolors, and bronze sculptures. His careful attention to detail allows his work to stretch across time and topic, making him one of America's greatest Western artists.

Using $500 from his father and money from the probated estate of his mother, Charlie and Nancy initiated the construction of their two-story wood-framed home in Great Falls in 1900. Charlie expressed little fondness for the home and constructed a much more rustic log cabin studio next door. With few native logs available in Great Falls, he purchased red cedar telephone poles (still showing holes from climbers' spikes) and assembled a one-room work area heated by a stone fireplace and graced by a skylight in the gabled roof. From there he set about producing his most notable works—those associated with the latter part of his career—over a twenty-year period.

Over the years, an addition to the studio, the realignment of walkways, the removal of noncontributing outlying structures, and a complete relocation of the Russells' house on the grounds formed the basis for the historic site seen today. His house and studio were enshrined as an NRHP site in 1966. Eventually, the addition of an adjacent modern brick museum and art gallery yielded a pleasing historic campus occupying several lots. Today, the complex is a mecca for Russell fans and Western art aficionados who want to see where Russell lived and worked—and view examples of what he produced.

—PHOTO BY STEVE WOODRUFF

—PHOTO BY ALONZO ROSADO

49

TENTH STREET BRIDGE

47°31′20″N 111°17′22″W

On the Missouri River in Great Falls in Cascade County

Historic bridges combine function and beauty and nostalgia in varying measures, and the Tenth Street Bridge over the Missouri River in Great Falls blends all three exceptionally. It is Montana's oldest and longest (1,130 feet) reinforced concrete, open-spandrel, multiarch bridge. Concrete piers and ice-guard abutments penetrate the riverbed below and support the eight arches. It is the bridge that Great Falls grew up around.

The bridge was constructed in 1920, corresponding with the rapid rise of Great Falls as an agricultural and industrial hub of central Montana. It connected the residential and commercial sector of the city on the south bank to the industrial complex in Black Eagle on the north bank, including the enormous Anaconda Company's copper-concentrate refinery with its series of hydroelectric dams.

Paris Gibson, the town's founding father and first mayor, spearheaded the construction efforts. It was chiefly his energy, money, and influence that led to "a conveyance that connects us in spirit and commerce," according to the *Great Falls Tribune* in celebrating the bridge's completion in December of 1920. By then, Gibson, at ninety-one, was in declining health and confined to his home. In his final year his son kept him abreast of the bridge's construction stages. He lived just long enough to see it completed.

The future of the bridge has been the focus of much debate in Great Falls. Time, weather, and travel have resulted in considerable deterioration and concern for safety. It was closed in 1975 for repairs to the bridge deck. Then, in 1986, county officials mounted efforts to replace it with a new bridge with a different alignment. But spirited citizens have led a counter-effort to preserve the aging structure. While there is a growing movement to identify, protect, and promote the community's historic resources, the bridge's future remains uncertain. Meanwhile, the bridge's gracefully continuous arches steadfastly carry traffic over the muddy waters below, true to their original purpose. It was nominated to the NRHP in 1996.

50

GRAND UNION HOTEL

47°48′52″N 110°40′08″W

In Fort Benton in Chouteau County

The phone number for the historic Grand Union Hotel ends with 1882, commemorating the year it was built. There is ongoing debate about whether or not the Grand Union is the oldest operating hotel in Montana, but what's not debatable is that the hotel was built a little too late to tap into a stream of steady patrons. Fort Benton was a lively steamboat town, but by the time the hotel was completed, steamboat traffic on the upper Missouri River was in steep decline. The hotel also missed the fur trade era, the gold rushes, and most of the Indian conflicts. On top of that, it witnessed the historic winter of 1886–87 that scuttled the vast open-range cattle industry throughout Montana. Then, too, by the 1890s, nearly all the buffalo had been wiped out on the northern Great Plains, so hunters looking for a room were in short supply. In all, the hotel was constructed too late to participate in much of the town's most colorful and rowdy historical moments.

As if poor timing wasn't bad enough, when the Great Northern Railway constructed a spur line from Havre to Great Falls, it bypassed Fort Benton altogether, keeping its tracks to a level alignment on the bluffs above the town. Railroad tycoon James J. Hill purposely ordered that the tracks skirt the former riverboat capital of Montana. He was never one to like competing enterprises, and it is said that he pulled down the window curtains of his opulent coach car when traveling by Fort Benton.

The hotel's massive foundation is composed of granite blocks placed into an 8-foot-deep trench. The exterior is faced with over a half million red and yellow bricks made from clay found on the hillside east of town. Other unique architectural features of the original hotel included woodstoves in each of its sixty guest rooms, a bath house, an elaborate two-story outhouse, a saddle room, and a ladies parlor. The original roof featured over 1 mile of hand-soldered tinned copper sheets, each one an inch wide. Nearly all the building materials arrived by steamboat via the Missouri River from St. Louis and St. Paul, including the solid black walnut for the grand staircase. All the wooden trim and moldings were hand-carved with molding planes. The original building has been modified and altered over the years.

The structure has its oddities: the first floor is actually four separate brick buildings divided by fire walls. Because the masons used whole bricks of varying dimensions, the second floor has imperfect square corners and straight sight lines. As a consequence, the hotel is 8 inches wider in the front than at the back. The windows had to be hand formed and deliberately slanted, with the downriver side 3 to 4 inches higher than the upriver side. Throughout the upper floors, there is a clear slope to the flooring. All window casings have segmental, arched tops to accommodate

—PHOTO BY STEVE WOODRUFF

the variance. Oddly, the river-view windows are the plainest, smallest, and least ornamental of the building. There was no basement in the original hotel, only a root cellar, a boiler room installed in 1889, and a wine cellar. A secret spy chamber with a slotted viewing window overlooks the entrance, lobby, and registration desk; it enabled guards to oversee the transfer of gold and other valuables stored in the hotel's vault.

Over a period of many decades, the Grand Union Hotel tumbled into disrepair and neglect. Owner after owner made gallant stabs at becoming successful hoteliers, but badly needed capital, labor, and restorative efforts never seemed to arrive in sufficient quantities to bring the structure back to its early elegance. Bats and rats were often the only guests in the boarded-up building, and fallen bricks often littered the sidewalks around it. After years of vacancy and vandalism, the hotel was sold at a sheriff's sale in 1986 to satisfy debts accumulated by previous owners. The hotel's contents, antiques, furnishings, and art objects were stripped and sold at public auctions. It hemorrhaged its history, piece by piece.

Finally, in 1995, new owners, well capitalized and with a grand vision and a sensitivity for the building's place in Montana's history, enabled the hotel to assert its original feeling for time and place. A massive restoration project transformed the hotel into a destination point for tourists, history buffs, and locals. It took some time, but the old Grand Union found its voice. Taken altogether, the blend of modern appointments and refurbishing presents a stunning guest facility that draws deeply on its historic beginnings. It earned a place on the NRHP in 1976.

—PHOTO BY STEVE WOODRUFF

EPILOGUE

SNOWDEN BRIDGE

48°00'00.1"N 104°05'43.7"W

On the Missouri River in Richland County just east of North Dakota border

Seemingly out of nowhere, the Snowden Bridge rises abruptly above the murky Missouri River like a giant misplaced erector set in eastern Montana. Its twin towers still encase the massive concrete counterweights, ready to drop slowly and raise the movable span for steamboats and barges to pass underneath. Few ever did, though. Although the bridge achieved its triple purpose to provide a railroad span for Great Northern Railway trains, create a barrier-free passageway for riverboat traffic, and establish a motor vehicle route across the Missouri River, it proved out of place and out of time.

The Snowden Bridge was built in 1913 by the Union Bridge and Construction Company of Kansas City based on plans drawn up by engineer J. A. L. Waddell. The design was considered an improved version of the Halstead Street bridge in Chicago, which Waddell designed in 1894. By the time Snowden Bridge was built, the steamboat era on the upper Missouri River had come to its natural end, having declined through the late 1800s as railroads emerged as the chief mode of transportation. Thus, upon the bridge's completion, one of its main purposes, to serve as a brief portal for river traffic below, was no longer needed.

The bridge's vertical lift section was the longest in the nation when completed. A control house on top of the lift span contained a kerosene-powered engine capable of raising the span in thirty minutes, augmented by the slow downward pull of the concrete counterweights attached to the steel span. Unofficial records state that the span was raised fewer than twenty times. Several of those times were to allow barges to pass during the construction of Fort Peck Dam.

Snowden Bridge also carried vehicular traffic—*at the same time it functioned as a railroad bridge*! Planking allowed vehicles to drive over the top of the tracks, and drivers paid a toll for this privilege. Electric signals and a horn system alerted drivers if a train was approaching. If it sounds dangerous, it was. However, a 1981 study found the bridge "so dangerous, it was safe," because drivers were exceptionally careful when crossing. The powerhouse on top of the span was removed in 1943, ending the era of the giant drawbridge. Vehicle traffic continued to use the bridge until as late as 1985.

Snowden Bridge has not achieved NRHP status and is noted here as an example of the number of storied historic sites in Montana still to be considered for listing. Snowden Bridge, like so many other sites, are worthy of—and await—inclusion.

—PHOTO COURTESY LIBRARY OF CONGRESS

BIBLIOGRAPHY

This book relied heavily on the documentation included with the National Register of Historic Places nomination forms. That documentation can be found at: https://www.nps.gov/subjects/nationalregister/database-research.htm

Abbott, E. C., and Helena Huntington Smith. 1955. *We Pointed Them North: Recollections of a Cowpuncher*. Norman, OK: University of Oklahoma Press.

Atkinson, Gail Shay, and Jim C. Atkinson. 1981. *Kalispell Cornerstones: A Fascinating History of Twenty-Five Kalispell Homes*. Kalispell, MT: O'Neil Printers.

Axline, Jon. 2005. *Conveniences Sorely Needed: Montana's Historic Highway Bridges, 1860–1956*. Helena, MT: Montana Historical Society Press.

Axline, Jon. 1993. *Monuments above the Water: Montana's Historic Highway Bridges, 1860–1956*. Helena, MT: Montana Department of Transportation.

Axline, Jon. 2015. *Taming Big Sky Country: The History of Montana Transportation from Trails to Interstates*. Charleston, SC: The History Press.

Baumler, Ellen, and Dave Shors. 2002. *Lost Places, Hidden Treasures: Rare Photographs of Helena, Montana*. Helena, MT: Farcountry Press.

Caldwell, Charlotte. 2012. *Visions and Voices: Montana's One-Room Schoolhouses*. Clyde Park, MT: Barn Board Press.

Cheney, Roberta, and Clyde Erskine. 2000. *Music, Saddles and Flapjacks: Dudes at the OTO Ranch*. Missoula, MT: Mountain Press Publishing.

Cohen, Stan. 2004. *Montana's Grandest: Historic Hotels and Resorts of the Treasure State*. Missoula, MT: Pictorial Histories Publishing.

Davis, Carl M. 2019. *Six Hundred Generations: An Archaeological History of Montana*. Helena, MT: Riverbend Publishing.

Dean, Patty (Ed.). 2009. *Coming Home: A Special Issue Devoted to the Historic Built Environment and Landscapes of Butte and Anaconda, Montana*. Helena, MT: Drumlummon Institute.

Devoto, Bernard (Ed.). 1953. *The Journals of Lewis and Clark*. Boston: Houghton Mifflin.

Ferris, Robert G. (Ed.). 1975. *Lewis and Clark: Historic Places Associated with Their Transcontinental Exploration (1804–1806)*. Washington, DC: US Department of the Interior, National Park Service.

Fifer, Barbara. 2002. *Montana Mining Ghost Towns*. Helena, MT: Farcountry Press.

Fred, Earl. 2013. *Marysville, Montana: Its History and Its People*. Earl Fred.

Gildart, Robert C. 1985. *Montana's Missouri River*. Helena, MT.: Montana Magazine.

Graetz, Rick, and Susie Graetz. 2001. *Montana's Upper Missouri River Breaks National Monument: The Wild and Scenic Missouri*. Helena, MT: Northern Rockies Publishing.

Grant, Marilyn. 1998. *A Guide to Historic Virginia City*. Helena, MT: Montana Historical Society Press.

Haney, Chuck. 2006. *Big Sky Barns: Grand and Historic Barns of Montana*. Helena, MT: Riverbend Publishing.

Hassrick, Peter H. 1989. *Charles M. Russell*. New York: Abrams.

Hornaday, William T. 2002. *The Extermination of the American Bison*. Washington, DC: Smithsonian Institution Scholarly Press.

Jenks, Jim. 2007. *A Guide to Historic Bozeman*. Montana Mainstreets, vol. 7. Helena, MT: Montana Historical Society Press.

Johnson, Evalyn Batten (on behalf of the Thompson-Hickman County Library). 2011. *Virginia City*. Charleston, SC: Arcadia Publishing.

Koch, Elers. 1998. *Forty Years a Forester, 1903 to 1943*. Missoula, MT: Mountain Press Publishing.

Kresek, Ray. 1998. *Fire Lookouts of the Northwest*. Spokane, WA: Historic Lookout Project.

Lonnquist, Lois. 2006. *Fifty Cents an Hour: The Builders and Boomtowns of the Fort Peck Dam*. Helena, MT: MT Sky Press.

Maclean, Vicky. 2014. *A Home in the Woods: Montana's Westside Ranger Stations*. Vicky MacLean.

MacLean, Vicky. 2013. *Home on the Range: Montana's Eastside Ranger Stations*. Vicky MacLean.

Martin, Dale. 2018. *Ties, Rails, and Telegraph Wires: Railroads and Communities in Montana and the West*. Helena, MT: Montana Historical Society Press.

Mathews, Allan James. 2002. *A Guide to Historic Missoula*. Montana Mainstreets, vol. 6. Helena, MT: Montana Historical Society Press.

McDonald, James A. 1981. *Missoula Historical Resource Survey*, Historical Research Associates, Missoula, MT.

Melcher, Joan. 2009. *Montana Watering Holes: The Big Sky's Best Bars*. Guilford, CT: Globe Pequot.

Montana Place Names from Alzada to Zortman: A Montana Historical Society Guide. 2009. Helena, MT: Montana Historical Society Press.

Pace, Dick. 1970. *Golden Gulch: The Story of Montana's Fabulous Alder Gulch*. 2nd ed. Dick Pace.

Partoll, Albert J. 1939. "Fort Connah: A Frontier Trading Post, 1847–1871." *Pacific Northwest Quarterly* 30 (4): 399–415.

Peterson, Don. 2010. *Great Falls*. Charleston, SC: Arcadia Publishing.

Quivik, Fred. 1982. *Historic Bridges in Montana*. Washington, DC: Historic American Engineering Record.

Rains, Steve. 2013. *Fire Lookouts, Northwest Montana*. Hamilton, MT: Stoneydale Press.

Robison, Ken. 2009. *Fort Benton*. Charleston, SC: Arcadia Publishing.

Russell, John C. 2019. *Treasure State Tycoon: Nelson Story and the Making of Montana*. Helena, MT: Montana Historical Society Press.

Rutkow, Eric. 2012. *American Canopy: Trees, Forests, and the Making of a Nation*. New York: Scribner.

Vaughn, J. W. 1956. *With Crook at the Rosebud*. Harrisburg, PA: Stackpole Books.

Vichorek, Daniel N. 1987. *Montana's Homestead Era*. Helena, MT: Montana Magazine.

West, Elliott. 2009. *The Last Indian War: The Nez Perce Story*. United States: Oxford University Press.

Wilson, Gary A. 2006. *Honky-Tonk Town: Havre, Montana's Lawless Era*. Guilford, CT: TwoDot.

Wyckoff, William. 2006. *On the Road Again: Montana's Changing Landscape*. Seattle, WA: University of Washington Press.

INDEX

Adams, J. C., 72
Adams Stone Barn, 72–73
agriculture, 24, 49, 98
Alder Gulch, 62
Alta Ranger Station, 44–45
American craftsman, 66
American Fur Company, 6
Anaconda, 23, 66, 68
Anaconda Copper Mining Company, 68, 108
Anaconda Hotel, 62
Anaconda Smokestack, 68–69
archeological sites, 16
artists, 12, 100, 106
Assiniboine, Fort, 1, 28–29
Atlas Bar, 56
Augusta, 74
automobiles, 52, 84

banks, 1, 2, 24, 74
Bannack, 62, 87
Battle of the Little Big Horn, 14, 21
barns, 2, 47, 49, 72
bars, 2, 56, 76
Bear Creek Field, 58
Bears Paw Mountains, 28
Beaverhead County, 64
Berkeley Pit, 66
Biddle, Spencer Fullerton Baird, 54
Big Hole Battlefield National Monument, 2
Big Hole River, 64
Big Horn County, 20
Big Porcupine Creek, 26
Billings, 90
bison, 10, 26
Bitterroot Forest Reserve, 44
Bitterroot Mountains, 44
Bitterroot National Forest, 42, 44, 46
Bitterroot River, West Fork of, 44
Black Eagle, 108
Blackfeet Indians, 8, 28, 59
Blaine County, 14, 84
Blankenbaker, Virgil, 82
Bodmer, Karl, 12
bone beds, 10
Boulder, 40
Bozeman, 59, 61
Boseman, John, 59
Bozeman Pass, 59
bridges, 2, 3, 23, 24–25, 47, 49, 108, 112–13
British, 6
Broadwater County, 38
Broadwater Hotel, 40
buffalo, 10, 27, 26, 100, 109
buffalo jumps, 10
bunkhouses, 30, 54, 55, 64
Burgess Garage, 52–53
Burlington Northern, 76, 80
Butte, 62, 66–67, 104
Butte-Anaconda Historic District, 66–67

Canada, 14, 80, 100
Carbon County, 58
Carnegie Library, 98
Carroll College, 96
Cascade County, 10, 72, 104, 106, 108
Cathedral of St. Helena, 96–97
Catholic Diocese, 96
cattle, 38, 54, 55, 59, 72, 82, 90, 94, 109
caves, 16
Cedar Creek, 94
cemeteries, 50,
Charles M. Russell House, 106–7
Cheney, Roberta, 94
Cheyenne Indians, 20
Chicago, Milwaukee, and St. Paul Passenger Depot, 104–5
Chico Hot Springs, 92–93
Chico School, 92
Chief Joseph, 14
Chief Joseph Battleground of the Bear's Paw, 14–15
Chinook, 14, 84
Chouteau County, 12, 30, 82, 109
churches, 2, 24, 70, 71, 88, 96, 97
Citadel Rock, 12–13
Civil War, 49
Civilian Conservation Corps, 46, 47
Clark, William, 12, 18
Clark Fork River, 98
coal mining, 49, 58
Comertown, 50–51
Connor, 44
Conrad, Charles, 100
Conrad Mansion, 100–101
cookhouses, 54
Coolidge, 64–65
Coolidge, Calvin, 64
copper, 40, 49, 66, 68, 109
Corps of Discovery, 8. *See also* Lewis and Clark Expedition
Cottonwood Creek Bridge, 2, 24–25
courthouse, 1, 2, 23, 40
Cover, Tom, 59
Craftsman, 66, 102
Crazy Horse, 20, 21
Crook, George, 20
Cross Ranch Headquarters, 54–55
Cruse, Thomas ,96
Custer, George A., 20

Davenport Hotel, 100
Dave's Texaco, 84–85
De Borgia, 46
Deaf and Dumb Asylum, 40
Dean School, 34–35
Deer Lodge County, 23, 68
Deer Lodge Valley, 68

depots, 49, 61, 74, 80–81, 94, 104–5
Depression, 25, 65, 88, 93, 94
De Smet, Pierre-Jean, 102
DeSmet tour boat, 102–3
Dillon, 87
disasters, 58
Dooley, 50
Droulliard, George, 8
dryland farming, 82
Drumlummon Mine, 70
dude ranches, 2, 94

Eagle Guard Station, 38
East Pioneer Mountains, 64
Elkhorn, 64–65
Elkhorn Mine, 64, 65
Emigrant, 92
Enlarged Homestead Act, 78
Essex, 76

Fallon County, 2, 24
Fergus County, 32
Fields, Joseph, 8
Fields, Reuben, 8
fire lookouts, 3, 23, 42
First Peoples Buffalo Jump, 10–11
Flathead County, 1, 76, 78, 100, 102
Flathead National Forest, 78
Flathead River, 76, 78
Flaxville, 50
forest rangers, 38, 44
forestry, 46
Forsyth, 56, 86
Fort Assiniboine, 1, 28–29
Fort Benton, 6, 12, 26, 30, 82, 100, 109
Fort Connah, 6–7
Fort Ellis, 59
Fort Peck, 88, 112
Fort Peck Dam, 88
Fort Peck Theatre, 88–89
Fort Shaw, 72
Froggie's Stopping Place, 2
fur trade, 5, 6, 12, 109

Gallatin County, 59
Gallatin National Forest, 94
Gallatin Valley, 59
garages, 2, 34, 52
Gardiner, 36, 94
Garnet, viii
Gardner River, 36
Garfield County, 26, 27
gas stations, 2, 84, 85
general stores, 50, 82
Georgian revival, 92
ghost town, viii, 62, 64
Gibson, A. J., 98
Gibson, Paris, 108
Gibsonb Mansion, 98
Gilman, 74
Gilman State Bank, 74–75
Gird Point Lookout, 42–43
Glacier National Park, 2, 3, 76, 102
gold mining, viii, 49, 59, 62, 70, 92, 109
Gothic, 96
grain elevators, 50, 61, 80
Grand Union Hotel, v, 109–11
Granite Peak, 46
Great Burn of 1910, 46
Great Depression, 25, 65, 88, 93, 94
Great Falls, 40, 74, 82, 104, 105, 106, 107, 108, 109
Great Northern Railway, 28, 56, 74, 76, 80, 82, 104, 109, 112
Great Sioux War, 20
Greenough, 98
Grinnell, George B., 100

Hackney, John S., 92
Haugen, 46
Havre, 28, 82, 109
Hayden, Ferdinand, 5
Helena, 38, 40, 62, 72, 96
Helena National Forest, 38
Hi-Line, 80, 84
Hill, James J., 100, 109
Hill County, 28

Historic Preservation Office, v
Homestead Era, 50, 52, 78, 82
homesteaders, 30, 49, 50, 52, 78, 82
Hornaday, William T., 26, 27
Hornaday Camp, 26–27
hospitals, 28, 40, 62, 88, 92, 93
hotels, 40, 62, 76–77, 109–11
hot springs, 36, 92, 93
Hudson's Bay Company, 6
Hughes Creek, 44
hunter-gatherers, 5

Indians. *See* Native Americans
industry, 24, 49, 54, 58, 82, 84, 94, 98, 109
Ingomar, 56
Ismay, 24
Izaak Walton Inn, 76–77

J. C. Adams Stone Barn, 72–73
jails, 23, 30, 31
Jefferson, Thomas, 8, 9, 49
Jefferson County, 40
Jersey Lilly Saloon, 56–57
Johnson, Charles, 98
Judith Landing Historic District, 5

Kalispell, 78, 100, 101
Kevin Depot, 80–81, 104
Koch, Elers, 46, 47

Lake County, 6
Lake McDonald Lodge, 100
Lambert, 2, 52
Last Chance Gulch, 62, 96
Late Victorian, 66
Leslie, Preston, 40
Lewis, Meriwether, 8
Lewis and Clark County, 70, 74, 96
Lewis and Clark Expedition, 5, 8, 12, 18
Lewistown, 32, 86
Lewistown Satellite Airfield, 32–33
lift bridge, 112

Lincoln, Abraham, 49
Little Powder River, 55
log cabins, 44, 66, 78, 94, 106
Lolo National Forest, 46
Lookout Cave, 16–17
lookouts, 3, 23, 42, 43

MacDonald, Angus, 6, 7
Madison County, 62
Marysville, 70, 96
Maximillian of Wied-Neuwied, 12
McDonald, Lake, 100, 102
Meade Hotel, 87
mercantiles, 59, 72, 82, 83
Methodist-Episcopal church, 70–71
Miles, Nelson, 14
Miles City, 24, 56
military, 14, 28, 32, 59
mills, 1, 20, 24, 49, 59, 61, 64, 65, 78
Milwaukee Railroad, 46, 56
Milwaukee Road, 104
Mineral County, 46
mining, vi, 49, 58, 62, 64, 65, 66, 68, 70, 92, 100
mining camps, 49, 65
missionary, 102
Missoula, 1, 46, 98, 104
Missoula County, 98
Missouri River, 5, 8, 12, 82, 104, 108, 109, 112
Montana Bar, 56
Montana Club, 40
Montana Southern Railway, 64
Montana State Training School, 40–41
Montana State University, 28, 61
Montana Stockgrowers Association, 54
Montana Territory, 26
Moss, Preston B., 90
Moss Mansion, 90–91
Mullan Road, 46, 47, 72
Museum of the Northern Great Plains, 26

National Park Service, 2, 14, 26
National Register of Historic Places, 1
Native Americans, 5, 6, 8–9, 10, 14–15, 16, 17, 20, 21
neoclassical, 98
New Deal, 88
Nez Perce, 14
Nez Perce National Historic Park, 14
1910 fire, 42
Norden bombsight, 32
Norman-style, 100
North Fork, 78
Northern Pacific Railway, 56, 59, 94, 104
Northern Pacific–Story Mill Historic District, 59–61

Oasis Bar, 56
oil, 2, 52, 80, 106
opera house, 62
OTO Dude Ranch, 94–95
Outlook, 50

Paris Gibson, 108
Park County, 36, 92, 94
Paulsen, John C., 40
Peterson, Gustav, 98
petroglyphs, 18
Phillips County, 16
Plentywood, 50
Pompeys Pillar, 18–19
Pondera County, 8
post offices, 23, 50, 52, 82, 92, 94
Powder River County, 54
Prahl, Emil and Sawtell, 24
Prohibition, 56, 93

Queen Anne, 66, 98

Radersburg, 38
railroads. *See* Burlington Northern; depots; Great Northern; Milwaukee; Northern Pacific
ranching, 54, 100
Randall, Dick and Nora, 94
ranger station, 2, 44
Rankin, Jeanette, 106
Ravalli County, 42, 44
Raymond, 50
Redstone, 50
Renaissance Revival, 66
resorts, 76, 92, 93
Richland County, 52, 112
rock art, 16
Rocky Boy's Indian Reservation, 28
Rocky Mountain College, 90
Roosevelt, Teddy, 36, 92
Roosevelt Arch, 36–37, 92
Rosebud Battlefield, 20–21
Rosebud County, 56
Rosebud Creek, 20, 21
Russell, Charles M., 92, 100, 106, 107

Saddleback Mountain, 64
Saltese, 46
Sapphire Mountains, 42
Savenac Nursery, 46–47
schoolhouses, 30, 34, 35
Sentinel, Mt., 98
settlement, 49, 59
Sheridan County, 50
silver mining, 49, 64, 65, 70
Silver Bow County, 66
silviculture, 46, 47
Sioux, 14, 20
smelters, 49, 68
Smith Mine, 58
Snake Creek, 14
Snowden Bridge, 112–13
Soo branch, 50
Sperry, Lyman B., 100
Square Butte Jail, 30–31
St. Ignatius, 6
statehood, 40, 49, 87
Statuary Hall, 106
steamboats, 112
Stillwater County, 34
Story, Nelson, 59, 61
Story Mill Historic District, 59–61
Sun River, 72, 74
Swiftcurrent lookout, 3

Taft, 46
Tenth Street Bridge, 108
territorial capitol, 62
Teton County, 1
Texas Trail, 54
theatres, 88, 89
Theodore Roosevelt International Highway, 84
timber, 3, 24, 25, 42, 44, 46, 49, 72
Toole County, 80
tourism, 62
Townsend, 38
train stations. *See* depots
trappers, 5, 12
Tudor revival, 76
Tuttle, Henry, 44
Two Medicine Fight Site, 8–9
Two Medicine River, 8

Ulm, 10
Ulm Pishkun Buffalo Jump State Park, 10–11
Union Bridge and Construction Company, 112
University Apartments, 1, 98–99
University of Montana, 98
US Forest Service, 38, 39, 44, 65

Valley County, 88
Victorian, late, 66
vigilante, 62
Virgelle Mercantile, 82–83
Virginia City, 62–63

Waddell, J. A. L., 112
Westby, 50
West Point, 21
wildfires, 42, 46
Wilkerson, Nathaniel, 44
Wise River, 64, 65
Works Progress Administration, 50, 88
World War I, 78, 82
World War II, 10, 25, 32, 58
Wurtz, Frank and Ella, 78
Wurtz Homestead, 38, 78–79

Yellowstone County, 18, 90
Yellowstone National Park, 36, 92, 94
Yellowstone River, 18, 26, 56, 59

MICHAEL J. OBER is four generations deep into Montana's history and lore. Born in Havre, Montana, he graduated from the University of Montana with a bachelor's degree in American history and English and, later, earned a master's degree in history at the university studying under the late K. Ross Toole. He also holds a master's of library and information science from the University of Denver. He has served as director of library services at Flathead Valley Community College for forty years, where he also taught Montana history. Seasonally, he worked as a wildland firefighter and backcountry ranger and law enforcement ranger in Glacier National Park for forty-four years. He is the author of *Glacier Album*, a showcase of vintage photographs of Glacier National Park, and numerous articles about Montana's culture and history in state and regional periodicals.